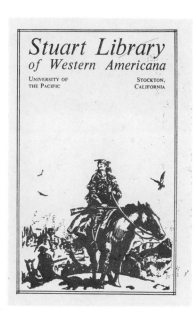

The Willamette Valley

MIGRATION AND SETTLEMENT ON THE OREGON FRONTIER

William A. Bowen is associate professor of geography at California State University, Northridge.

The Willamette Valley

MIGRATION AND SETTLEMENT ON THE OREGON FRONTIER

William A. Bowen

UNIVERSITY OF WASHINGTON PRESS   Seattle and London

Copyright © 1978 by the University of Washington Press
Printed in the United States of America

This book was published with the assistance of a grant from
the Andrew W. Mellon Foundation.

Library of Congress Cataloging in Publication Data
Bowen, William A., 1941–
  The Willamette Valley.

  Bibliography: p.
  Includes index.
  1. Willamette Valley—History. 2. Frontier
and pioneer life—Oregon—Willamette Valley. I. Title.
F882.W6B68   979.5'3'03   77-15183
ISBN 0-295-95590-2

Dedicated with love to my parents,

William and Marie,

my wife, Marilyn,

and our children, Wendy and Billy

Acknowledgments

I WISH to thank all those whose help and interest made the research for this book a pleasant experience: Professors James Parsons and Gunther Barth of the University of California, Berkeley, for their early encouragement; Miss Linda Bowen for her typing of the original manuscript and computer programming; Mr. Larry Miyaki, who assisted with the final cartography; and the many staff members of the Bancroft Library, Oregon Historical Society, Oregon State Archives, University of Oregon Library, and the Portland office of the United States Bureau of Land Management. A special thanks is owed to William and Eva Bowen of Portland, Oregon. Their generous hospitality sustained me through a very wet winter.

Contents

Introduction   3

1. Physical Landscape and Historical
   Background   6

2. Motivation and Migration   17

3. Sources of Information about the
   Oregon Frontier   22

4. The Localization of Settlement in Oregon   43

5. Physical Environment and Settlement   59

6. Frontier Economy and Land   65

7. The Farm and Rural Economy   73

8. Frontier Agriculture   79

9. Conclusion   95

Appendix: Cartographic Resources and
   Mapping the 1850 Census   97

Notes   105

Bibliography   107

Index   119

Illustrations

MAPS

1. Pacific Northwest   4

2. Major Streams and Topographical Features   7

3. Willamette Valley Settlements, 1811–1841   8

4. Willamette Valley Settlements, 1850–1855   13

5. Oregon Counties, 1850   15

6. American Population of Oregon   27

7. Origins and Destinations of Oregon Immigrants Passing through Missouri   34

8. Origins and Destinations of Oregon Immigrants Passing through Illinois   35

9. Origins and Destinations of Oregon Immigrants Passing through Iowa   36

10. Diffusion of New York Families Migrating to Oregon   37

11. Diffusion of Virginia Families Migrating to Oregon   38

12. Diffusion of Kentucky Families Migrating to Oregon   39

13. Counties of Birth and Marriage of Oregon Donation Land Claims Recipients   41

14. Households Containing Persons Born in Canada   44

15. Households Containing Persons Born in Foreign Countries   44

16. Households Containing Persons Born in New England   45

17. Households Containing Persons Born in Middle Atlantic States   45

18. Households Containing Persons Born in Ohio   47

19. Households Containing Persons Born in South Atlantic States   47

29. Households Containing Persons Born in Kentucky   48

21. Households Containing Persons Born in Tennessee   48

22. Households Containing Persons Born in Indiana   49

23. Households Containing Persons Born in Illinois   49

24. Households Containing Persons Born in Iowa   51

25. Households Containing Persons Born in Missouri   51

26. Willamette Valley Kinship Ties   52

27. Four Associated Family Clusters   54

28. Age-Sex Characteristics of County Populations   57

29. Age-Sex Characteristics of Urban Centers   57

30. Willamette Valley Prairies, 1851–1856   60

31. Oregon Population, 1850   61

32. Sawmills and Gristmills   63

33. Beef Cattle   81

34. Milch Cows   82

35. Working Oxen   84

36. Horses   85

37. Sheep   86

38. Swine   88

39. Wheat   89

40. Oats   90

41. Peas and Beans   91

42. Irish Potatoes   92

43. Value of Market Garden Produce   93

44. Census Marshal's Route   99

45. Oregon City Land Office Cadastral
    Survey Plat   102

FIGURES

1. Oregon Population, 1850   55

2. Population Pyramids: Oregon, 1850   56

3. 1850 Population Census Schedule   98

4. 1850 Agriculture Census Schedule   100

5. 1850 Agriculture Census Schedule
   (second page)   101

Tables

1. Oregon Census, 1845   14

2. Territorial Census, 1849   14

3. Oregon Population by Place of
   Origin, 1850   25

4. Michael Shelly Family   28

5. Individual Migration   30

6. Family Migration   32

7. Relative Importance of Heartlands as
   Reflected in Kinship Ties   40

8. Urban Population by State or Region
   of Origin   46

9. Map Location Accuracy of Rural
   Population   103

The Willamette Valley

MIGRATION AND SETTLEMENT ON THE OREGON FRONTIER

Introduction

IN THOSE PARTS of the world long occupied by diverse and technologically advanced cultures, it is usually difficult, if not impossible, to unravel the origins of the often confusing array of forms that comprise a cultural landscape. The anonymity of distant history drains men of their humanity, making them over into faceless tribes whose pioneering and early development of the land lie hidden in the fading mists of time.

In North America, however, the study of culture's impress on the earth is simplified, for the confrontation between Neolithic and modern Western civilizations was recent, abrupt, and extensively documented. Except for the more advanced native societies of the Southwest, most of the continent was inhabited by tribes of hunters and gatherers or agriculturalists that were quickly swept aside wherever the invaders wished to occupy the land. Little of the old cultures was lastingly assimilated by the new. A few domesticated crops, place names, and subtly altered natural environments were about all that were incorporated into it.

Less than two centuries have elapsed since the American frontier crossed the Alleghenies and much less since the transformation of the trans-Missouri west began, yet it is already difficult to bridge the narrow gap of time and picture with any accuracy the land as it was, to measure the first tentative steps of settlement. Fact and fancy intermingle to form imaginative and sometimes imaginary landscapes, and mythical abstractions substitute too often for knowledge.

Even in many of our most studied districts, little can be said with certainty about the land and the great majority of plain people whose success or failure in everyday life determined the course of western development. Literally thousands of books have been written about the romantic, marvelous aspects of the American West, but what of the ordinary? Exactly who were the legendary, and yet unknown, masses that formed the sinew of the new societies? From where did they come,

and why? How did they meet the challenge of a wilderness in order to survive and prosper?

One way these and other crucial questions may be answered is through reconstruction of past landscapes. Although time-consuming, this is not an impossible task when directed at infant communities with limited populations. Computers allow a single person to track the thousands of individual histories that together record the workings of a society, and maps permit a sophisticated, yet elegantly simple, presentation of the results.

The area and period chosen for investigation is Oregon, south of the Columbia River, during the 1840s. No other far western frontier, with the possible exception of California, so captured the imagination of the American public at the time. In many ways Oregon became a focal point for the romance and legends associated with the West. The ponderous ox-drawn wagons making their long summer crossing, the people, the herds, and the sometimes terrible suffering all embody the hallowed spirit of a westering nation. In the minds of most Americans the Oregon Trail ranks in importance with such national shrines as Plymouth Rock, Bunker Hill, and the Alamo.

Folklore aside, the Oregon frontier has many virtues that recommend it to those who would better understand life on the margins of civilization. To this distant land the first great overland migrations of continental dimensions directed their course. There, in the lush, green valleys south of the Columbia River and west of the Cascade Range, the first sizable Anglo-American settlement was established on the Pacific Coast, a colony that enjoyed primacy until overshadowed by the California Gold Rush.

By 1850, when the first period of immigration was complete, settlement had spread throughout the Willamette Valley and to the coastal lands immediately south of the mouth of the Columbia River (map 1). Altogether approximately four thousand square miles lay within the frontier, and according to the United States census of that year,

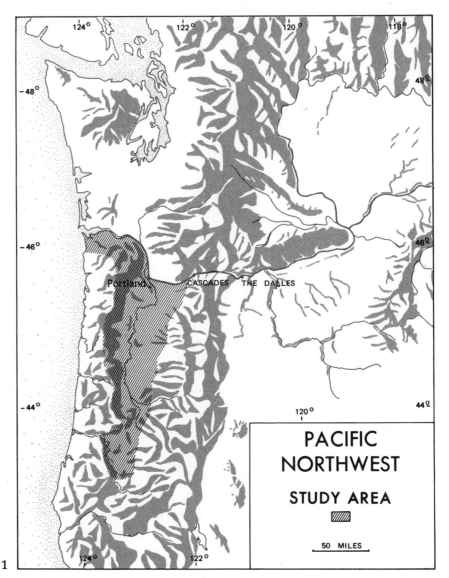

MAP 1

the population numbered some twelve thousand persons. Men from many states and nations came to Oregon, but the majority were natives of the great Mississippi Valley, farmers who with their families and friends crossed the plains in search of new and better homes. Some followed the siren calls of adventure and profit. Many others pursued the illusive promise of good health. But, whatever their origins or motivations, they created a major western frontier, a colony which incorporated within its structure both the worldliness of a cosmopolitan urban society and the provincialism of rural America.

At mid-century the size and complexity of the settlement were already sufficiently great to con-

found simple generalization. As a result, the main thrust of this work is aimed at what might be called the "common frontier experience." Conscious effort is made to concentrate on typical, rather than unique, aspects of the land, the people, and their resulting interaction. Although their presence is recognized, foreign minorities are largely passed over in favor of the American-born. Town dwellers, likewise, are subordinated to the bulk of the population that lived on farms.

This is an atlas—a collection of extremely detailed, accurate maps with text that, for the first time, re-creates the essential geography of a major American frontier in the nineteenth century. It is not another regional history that attempts to breathe new life into old stories. Neither is it simply a treatise on frontier process, migration, or settlement, although all these subjects are explored. Location is the central theme, its description and explanation. The map is the primary form of expression.

CHAPTER 1

Physical Landscape and Historical Background

In 1850, the Oregon Country included a vast territory stretching westward from the Rocky Mountains between the forty-second and forty-ninth parallels. Within its borders lay more than a quarter million square miles of plateau and mountain, over which men from distant nations had long pursued fortune. Little of consequence awaited discovery. Both Englishmen and Americans had navigated the Columbia River and its tributaries, traded with the Indians, and settled. Yet, by mid-century the land remained hardly touched. In the interior, east of the great Cascade Range, a few fortified trading posts and recently abandoned missions testified to the invaders' tenuous hold over the country. On the precipitous, fog-enshrouded coast neither fishermen nor loggers plied their trades, and the wet, forested expanses of the Coast and Cascade ranges remained a *terra incognita*. Only along the lower course of the Columbia River and in the Willamette Valley to the south had the newcomers made a lasting mark. Here was the settled frontier, the land men thought of when they spoke of Oregon.

Between the Cascades and the Coast Range, isolated from both the arid interior and the rainy coast, lies the Willamette Valley, heart of the Old Oregon Country (map 2). The broad structural lowland is approximately one hundred miles long by twenty to thirty miles wide and is divided by low intervening hills into several more or less well-defined sections.

Southernmost and largest of these is a spacious alluvial plain located south of the Santiam River. Except for a number of small volcanic buttes situated back from the left bank of the South Santiam, this upper half of the valley is an open, level country once occupied by a great grassland. The Willamette River and its tributary, the McKenzie, flow northward across the plain, joining to form a seasonally inundated strip of meandering, complexly braided channels, riverine woodlands, and marshes.

Below the junction of the Willamette and San-tiam rivers, forested hills interrupt the valley's flat floor. The Waldo Hills, a rolling upland some five to eight hundred feet high, are the lowest and most extensive. Farther west the slightly higher Croisan Ridge and oak-covered Eola Hills press in on either side of the now slightly entrenched main stream.

Beyond the intersecting ridges the valley's floor flattens once more. With increasing frequency, however, it is broken by high, wooded ground. Along the Willamette's west bank, the Eola Hills separate the Yamhill River plains from those to the east. Northward, the Chehalem and Tualatin mountains extend across the lowland to almost completely encircle the two hundred square mile Tualatin Valley and isolate the main valley from the Columbia River. Forested hills impinge on the Willamette River and the heretofore placid current races forward until it plunges over a thirty-foot-high lava sill, shaking the earth in its descent. Downstream lie the great terraces and marshes of the Columbia River.

The valley's climate and flora reflect its near coastal location, midway between equator and pole. To the south is the warm, stable air of the subtropical high, while to the north are the cool, stormy North Pacific westerlies. As these two dissimilar atmospheric systems follow the sun's seasonal migration, the land is subject alternately to cloudy and clear weather. During the long wet season between September and April, storms sweep in from the sea in rapid succession, drenching the Willamette with forty to fifty inches of rainfall each year. In the surrounding mountains, the annual total often exceeds twice that amount, and above three thousand feet much of this falls as snow.

Because of the valley's proximity to the Pacific Ocean, temperatures seldom reach uncomfortable extremes. Monthly means range from a July maximum in the middle to upper sixties to a January low in the upper thirties. Rare days may witness thermometers climbing above one hundred degrees Fahrenheit or skidding to below zero, but the norm is a coolish fifty or sixty degrees under cloudy skies.

At the time of the first migrations, a great forest of Douglas fir, incense cedar, hemlock, spruce, and fir clothed the lower mountain slopes of western Oregon. In the lower, drier Willamette Valley, the dark monotony of these tall trees gave way to open white oak savannas and, on the level plains, grass. Southward from the Pudding River progressively larger, tree-fringed prairies carpeted the rich alluvial soil. This was the good land, the land of Oregon.

Commercial organizations, not governments or individuals, dominated the formative years of economic development in the Pacific Northwest. Furs provided the incentive for organizing companies, and the requirements of trade controlled both exploration and settlement. A Boston trading ship, the *Columbia Rediviva* commanded by Captain Robert Gray, first entered and gave her name to the mightiest of the continent's Pacific rivers. A New York firm, John Jacob Astor's Pacific Fur Company, financed Astoria, Oregon's first successful colony.

Begun in 1811 and completed the following year, Astoria was to be the cornerstone in the Pacific Fur Company's plan for absolute trade monopoly over the coast and the interior. To accomplish this objective in an economic manner, a site was chosen near the mouth of the Columbia River on the first high ground along the south bank (map 3). There, above a protected cove, employees erected fortifications and laid out a small garden.

The location had much to offer trading firms dependent on shipborne supplies. From it the Astorians could regulate traffic along the river and thereby the inland trade; control one of the best anchorages and hence dominate the coastal business; provide warehousing facilities for both interior and coastal trade; and operate a retail outlet for local Indians. True, the rocky, heavily timbered ground proved to be less than ideal for agriculture, but so long as the original plan to import food by ship could be implemented this was not a serious handicap.

Geography alone could not sustain the enterprise in the face of unforeseen disasters. Destruction of the ship *Tonquin*, her crew, and supplies, the North West Fur Company's entry into the chosen domain, and the War of 1812 combined to defeat Astor's venture. Yet, the settlement

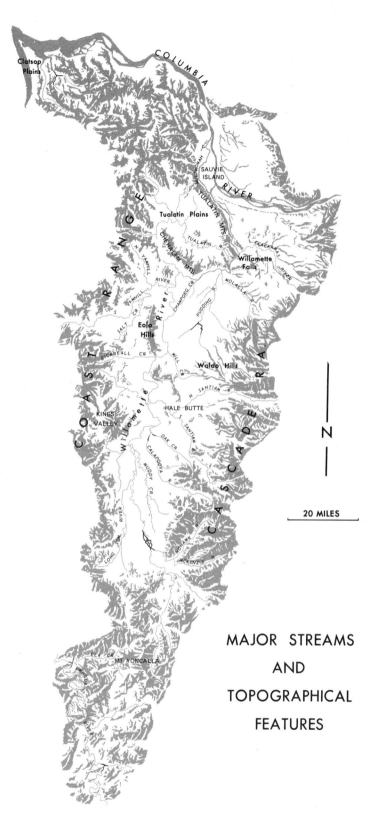

MAJOR STREAMS

AND

TOPOGRAPHICAL

FEATURES

MAP 2

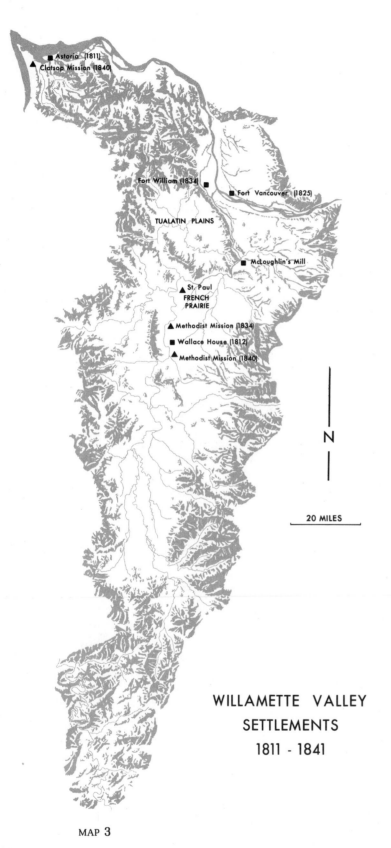

Astoria (1811)
Clatsop Mission (1840)

Fort William (1834)
Fort Vancouver (1825)

TUALATIN PLAINS

McLoughlin's Mill

St. Paul
FRENCH
PRAIRIE

Methodist Mission (1834)
Wallace House (1812)
Methodist Mission (1840)

N

20 MILES

WILLAMETTE VALLEY
SETTLEMENTS
1811 - 1841

MAP 3

remained, as did more than a dozen of its original inhabitants. The new company's needs differed little from its predecessor's, and the function and substance of the fort remained unchanged.

Inland, the activities of the two companies assumed a more transient character. Clerks of the Pacific Fur Company erected a trading house in the upper Willamette Valley as early as November 1812, and at least two other establishments were built within several miles of the present site of Newberg. All, however, were little more than temporary encampments. The importance of the early trading ventures to settlement lay in their stimulation of public interest in Oregon and the support they provided newly arrived individuals on this farthest frontier, not in the size or number of their installations.

Assimilation of the North West Fur Company by the Hudson's Bay Company in 1821 presaged change in trading practices. Determined that the Columbia District should become independent of imported foodstuffs, and finding Astoria unsuited for agriculture, Sir George Simpson, governor of the Honorable Company, ordered the regional headquarters moved in 1825. The new establishment was named Fort Vancouver and was located one hundred miles upstream on the Columbia, nearly opposite the mouth of the Willamette River. The status of Astoria, or Fort George as it had been renamed by the British, rapidly declined to that of a communication station and local trading post. Henceforth, settlement would focus on the interior instead of the coast.

Unlike his predecessors, Chief Factor John McLoughlin was required by company policy to occupy much of his time with the development of a large agricultural enterprise. Besides the construction of the usual fortified post, herds of livestock had to be established, mills for sawing lumber and grinding wheat had to be built, and the land had to be cleared, fenced, and cultivated. With the passing years the fort assumed more the appearance of a farming community than that of a fur trading establishment. While the palisade, the warehouses, and shops continued to belie the colony's primary function, visitors commented with increasing frequency upon the post's ancillary agricultural activities.

Within four years of his arrival on the Columbia, McLoughlin faced a serious problem, concerning some of the company's older servants who had originally come to the coast with the Pacific Fur Company. After the British acquisition of Astoria, most of these men joined the service of the North West Company and had in turn been employed by the Hudson's Bay Company. Under the latter corporation's charter, retired personnel had to be repatriated back to the country from which they joined, usually Lower Canada or the British Isles. Normally this arrangement was mutually satisfactory, for the employee received a free passage home and the company preserved its authority over all whites within its jurisdiction. In the case of the Astorians, however, the men, predominantly French Canadian, had enlisted in Oregon. During their long residence, they had married Indian women and raised families, and they now asked to remain and start farms. The request was not easily turned aside, for if the men left, their numerous half-breed children would have been cut off from the influence of the company and raised as Indians. Experience had shown how difficult it was to deal with such offspring, and in view of the number of persons who would be eventually involved, the possibilities for suffering and discontent were great.

Recognizing the problem and realizing that it could be turned to the company's advantage, the chief factor subverted the regulations and at the same time maintained his authority over the men by retaining them technically in the employ of the corporation. Then he subsidized their initial efforts by lending them livestock and seed and by selling necessities at reduced rates. All this was done on the proviso that the men should go to the Willamette Valley, where isolated from tribal influence their children could be raised as whites friendly to the company, and where the children and their mothers would serve as hostages for the good conduct of their Indian relatives.

During the years following 1829, most of the French Canadians established farms in what was to become known as the "French District," or French Prairie, a grassland between the Willamette and Pudding rivers. A few families settled along the west bank of the Willamette, and still others located on the Scappoose Plains, near the Columbia River opposite the lower end of Sauvie Island. Within a short time, French Prairie became a small but thriving agricultural settlement. Wheat harvests were large enough to require the erection of a warehouse at Champoeg, and by 1841 the number of families had increased to sixty-one, with an attendant population of about three hundred and fifty persons.

Meanwhile, an irregular but increasing trickle of newcomers began to enter the valley. Itinerant bands of American trappers, tourists, and government agents visited the frontier, leaving behind a few new volunteers, but without adequate resources none could effectively challenge continuing British dominance. This situation began to change only when, in 1834, Methodist missionaries reached the Willamette Valley under the protection of Nathaniel Wyeth, a Yankee trader.

The Reverend Jason Lee and his associates were men of unimpeachable character who did not threaten the Hudson's Bay Company's monopoly, and as a result, they were taken in and assisted in their enterprise by McLoughlin. In retrospect, the chief factor's good intentions seem unwarranted, for although the Methodist Mission was a charitable institution founded on Christian principles, it was also an organization with resources not unlike those of any corporation. For instance, it had an absentee board of directors. Mission personnel were salaried employees, and like the traders they could depend upon outside sources of supply and economic subsidy. Initially there was the important difference that the missionaries labored to save souls, while the traders worked for profits. Even this distinction, however, soon disappeared.

Among the Americans, farming was considered a vital force in civilizing and Christianizing Indians. This belief plus the obvious agricultural potential of the Willamette Valley so impressed Jason Lee that he decided to establish his mission in the vicinity of the French settlement, instead of in the distant Flathead country as had been originally planned. The site chosen was on the low alluvial lands of the Willamette River's east bank, several miles southwest of the retired Canadians.

The Methodist Mission never became a philanthropic success. From the beginning, disease and the natives' dislike of manual labor doomed the enterprise to failure. Nevertheless, its establishment did result in frequent communication with the United States and an influx of settlers independent of British control. Within three years approximately thirty whites were attached to the project, and many of these had spread out from the original compound to occupy nearby farms.

The rate of growth did not satisfy Superintendent Lee, who from 1838 onward increasingly became a publicist and speculator in the eyes of his detractors. That year he returned to the United States and conducted a lecture tour through the

Mississippi Valley and New England espousing Oregon settlement. As a result of his efforts, another fifty-two persons were sent out on the ship *Lausanne* in 1840. Eventually the Methodist Board of Missions supported more than seventy Americans in the country.

With the addition of reinforcements colonization began in earnest. The first decision was to move the main mission compound. The original site had always been plagued by disease, and now it proved too restrictive to grand schemes. Lee chose a more suitable location at Chemeketa, on the east bank of the Willamette about ten miles upstream from the old mission. New buildings were erected there, fields enclosed, and a grist mill built.

Earlier in 1838 Daniel Lee and H. K. W. Perkins had founded the Wascopam Mission at The Dalles, east of the Cascade Range on the south bank of the Columbia River. Now, with the aid of his latest recruits, Jason Lee started two more missions at strategic, outlying points—one on Puget Sound near Fort Nisqually and the other on the Clatsop Plains, below the mouth of the Columbia.

While establishing these satellite stations, the Methodists became embroiled in the famous dispute with John McLoughlin over ownership of the Willamette Falls and adjacent lands. In the summer of 1840, Alvan Waller erected a building on the east bank of the river near the cascades to function as a home and store. In 1841 he was joined by Felix Hathaway, who began building on the small island in the middle of the falls. McLoughlin, whose prior claim to the land and whose plans for developing a mill and town were threatened, retaliated by surveying town lots and selling them against the Methodists' wishes. Litigation would continue for years, but for Oregon City, the frontier's infant metropolis, development had begun.

Jason Lee's Oregon experiment ended abruptly in 1844. Upon being informed of the increasingly secular nature of the enterprise, the Methodist Board of Missions recalled the superintendent and closed the mission, turning over its property to those members who wished to remain in the country. Inasmuch as all but one of the laymen were determined to stay, most of the church's assets passed into their hands at a nominal cost. Hamilton Campbell purchased the mission's cattle herds on long-term credit, and George Abernethy obtained the store at the falls. The mission at The Dalles was sold to Marcus Whitman, and those

on the Clatsop Plains and at Nisqually were discontinued.

The only other Protestant effort in the Willamette Valley occurred on the West Tualatin Plains, where in 1840 and 1841 Congregational and Presbyterian missionaries settled after failing in their labors among the tribes of eastern Oregon. An attempt was made to found a mission school for local Indians, but it was soon abandoned, the personnel becoming farmers like their Methodist brethren.

More important than the lesser Protestant sects was a third group of religious colonizers, the Roman Catholics. As early as 1836, the residents of French Prairie had petitioned the Bishop of Juliopolis in Canada to send priests. Not until two years later, however, could two candidates be found and their passage secured on the Hudson's Bay Company express from Red River. They were Father Francis N. Blanchet from Lower Canada and the Reverend Modeste Demers of Juliopolis.

After several months Father Blanchet established a parish on French Prairie, where the Canadians had anticipated the priest by erecting, in 1836, a log church about four miles south of Champoeg. This structure was dedicated to Saint Paul on January 6, 1840, and the work of the Roman Catholic Church began in western Oregon. The priest's efforts were soon amply rewarded, for he was surrounded by men who had been brought up in his faith. Much to the disgust of the Methodists, the Indians also found the mystical qualities of the Roman Church more attractive than the abstract plainness of the Protestants and the labor they required.

Unlike the Methodists, the priests and nuns never contributed significantly to the growth of the population or actively attempted to induce settlement. Their contribution was not so much a quantitative one as it was a factor in the qualitative distribution of population. Before the Church's coming, the French Canadians had actively participated in the general society of the valley. They had helped the Methodists. They had contributed their money and energy in combination with others to bring cattle from California, and they had even supposedly participated in memorials sent to the United States Congress. After Father Blanchet's arrival all this changed, and increasingly the French Prairie settlers segregated themselves from those who surrounded them. Cultural differences augmented by religious division quickly led to the development of a closed ethnic community, isolated from the main stream of frontier society and politics.

One other type of organization subsidized settlement in Oregon besides the trading companies and missions. That was the Puget Sound Agricultural Company, a subsidiary of the Hudson's Bay Company organized in the late 1830s to provide farm products for the Russians in Alaska in exchange for territorial concessions along the north coast. For years a difference of opinion existed within the directorship of the Hudson's Bay Company concerning the propriety and economic sense of a trading firm based on furs engaging in large scale commercial agriculture. To resolve the difficulty and increase production to levels required by the new Russian agreement, the company issued a prospectus outlining a separate corporation to be founded under the auspices of the parent company. Capitalized at two hundred thousand pounds sterling, the junior firm was to purchase all livestock and agricultural implements of the parent and establish commercial farms. Despite this maneuver, the corporate independence of the Puget Sound Agricultural Company was more technical than real. Its personnel operated under the laws of the Hudson's Bay Company. Its manager was that company's chief factor on the Northwest Coast. Its shares were owned almost entirely by Hudson's Bay Company stockholders, and its directors came from that corporation's board of directors.

Although the corporate entity was something of a fiction, its new policy was not. The company proposed to systematically settle the country north of the Columbia River between the mouth of the Cowlitz River and Puget Sound—not to trade with the Indians, not to Christianize them, but to colonize. Agricultural settlement would be a primary goal, not a useful adjunct to other pursuits. To this end herds and implements of the company's posts were turned over to the new firm. In addition, large herds of cattle and sheep were brought overland from California. Swine and improved breeds of sheep were imported from England, and more importantly, knowledgeable farmers and shepherds were brought with their families from the British Isles and Canada.

In the fall of 1841, twenty-one of these families arrived north of the Columbia and began the work. Careful planning, experienced leadership and personnel, and sufficient capital, however, were not enough to insure the economic success of the enterprise. Neither did the ill-disguised attempt succeed in establishing a viable British colony and, through it, territorial control.

One of the great flaws in the plan was its failure to recognize the effect free land in the Willamette Valley would have on the new employees. Servants abandoned their poorly paying jobs and migrated south, where they settled on the French Prairie and the Tualatin Plains. To the advantage of the country south of the Columbia River, the only British attempt expressly calculated to establish an agricultural colony failed.

Not all those who traveled overland to Oregon were experienced in wilderness life. Undoubtedly, the worst conceived migration of the 1830s was made by the so-called "Peoria Party." This group originally consisted of eighteen young men from Peoria, Illinois, who, after hearing lectures by Jason Lee in the autumn of 1838, determined to go west in search of health and adventure. With the motto "Oregon or the Grave," the company set out in May 1839. Lack of experience and common purpose soon took their toll, and the party disintegrated into several quarrelsome cliques that straggled into Fort Vancouver during the next spring.

The misadventures of Thomas Farnham and his seventeen cohorts were of no greater importance and would hardly be worth noting, if they did not testify to the degree institutionally subsidized settlement had changed the Far West in less than thirty years. Where heavily armed, disciplined parties had once hardly dared travel, unprepared fools could now survive. Just as the fur companies and religious societies supported the construction of trading posts and missions, these settlements in turn could aid other travelers along the route to Oregon. At Fort Hall, Fort Boise, Waiilatpu, Lapawi, Fort Vancouver, and the Methodist Mission, Farnham and his associates found food, shelter, clothing, and even employment. These men were saved. Hundreds of others would be likewise assisted in the near future. To a significant degree both the overland route and the western Oregon frontier were prepared for a massive migration.

The first crossing of a family from the Missouri frontier overland to Oregon for the expressed purpose of settling and establishing a farm occurred in 1840. The family was that of Joel P. Walker, brother of the trapper and explorer Joseph R. Walker, and a frontiersman in his own right. Especially noteworthy was his use of wagons as far as Fort Hall, where others were preparing for the westward journey.

With the collapse of the fur trade American trappers were abandoning the Rocky Mountains for the Willamette Valley, taking their Indian families with them just as the retiring French Canadians had done. Unlike gentlemen travelers or the Canadians, they were neither refined tourists nor trusted and obedient servants of the British monopoly. They were free men from the western states, potentially violent, uncouth vagabonds. As far as the Hudson's Bay Company and the Methodists were concerned, there was no place for them on French Prairie or at Chemeketa. Only grudgingly would the missionaries even sell them potatoes.

Attempting to make the best of a poor situation, McLoughlin suggested to the American hunters that they settle on the plains adjacent to the Tualatin River, where there was sufficient open ground of good quality to sustain a farming community. There they were close to the watchful eyes of the chief factor and separate from the more stable elements of the valley's population. To ensure the men's propriety McLoughlin persuaded four representatives of the independent Congregational missions to settle among them.

By 1841 three important communities existed south of the Columbia River: the French Canadians on the prairie south of Champoeg, the Methodists upriver from them, and the free Americans at "Rocky Mountain Retreat" on the Tualatin Plains. Immigration that year added slightly more than one hundred persons to the population of these districts.

The following year, 1842, marked a turning point in the overland migration to Oregon. Until then independent crossings were at best sporadic and poorly organized, the participants few in number. Subsequently they would be continuous, and the number of individuals would be counted in the hundreds and thousands. Probably no more than one hundred and fifty persons were added to the population that year, but more than two-thirds of these came with Elijah White as members of the first typical wagon train to the Pacific Northwest.

In its outfit and organization the White train was little different from the caravans that had traveled to Santa Fe for two decades. At the same time, it was the prototype of those that would follow it over the Oregon Trail. In addition to oxen, horses, and pack mules, the train included cattle and eighteen large wagons. These were circled each evening in the traditional manner and the livestock corraled within the perimeter. Following the Santa Fe pattern, the membership hired guides and established an organization to maintain order and regulate daily tasks.

The train suffered from the same internal dissension that would plague subsequent emigrant parties. Indian scares, tedium, brief intermissions at Fort Laramie and Fort Hall, and final exhaustion of the party foreshadowed the experiences of future migrants. So also did their destitution.

To help alleviate the suffering the Methodists employed several men. A far greater number were hired by John McLoughlin, who also furnished the newcomers with food and other supplies on credit. Since the chief factor's personal economic interests centered on the development of a water power site at the falls of the Willamette River, his newly arrived employees could not scatter to isolated claims, but had to remain together near the mill. As a result, the 1842 migration contributed little to the frontier's existing rural population. Instead, it provided the nucleus of the frontier's first town, Oregon City (map 4). During the winter of 1842–43 the village on the east bank grew to almost thirty structures.

Every spring for the next five years an increasing multitude converged on the Missouri frontier. From St. Joseph, Independence, and other river towns they set forth on their memorable summer journeys. Much has been written of the adventure and suffering encountered by those who made the crossing, but for most the trip was just hard, dirty work.

Each year the details of the story changed, yet the common themes remained the same. Discomfort led to dissension and disorganization as family cliques or neighborhood groups severed themselves from the main bodies. Many did not fully comprehend the difficulties that lay beyond the Rocky Mountains. Discipline slackened, and progress slowed. Parties loitered or through miscalculation wore themslves out. In the end, most immigrants reached the Columbia exhausted and unequipped to face the rigors of the last several miles. The passage down the river canyon or over the mountains left nearly all as destitute as those who had preceded them.

The "Great Migration" of 1843 brought approximately eight hundred newcomers to the Willamette Valley, and the next year witnessed the addition of hundreds more. By the summer of

1845, an official census taken for the Provisional Government indicated more than two thousand persons resided south of the Columbia River. The majority of these, especially the more recent arrivals, were from the Middle West, and they showed their frontier condition in their youthfulness and a preponderance of men (table 1). Fully 48 percent of the inhabitants were less than eighteen years old, and of this group 78 percent were younger than twelve years. In contrast, only 7 percent of the total population were forty-five and older.

Males of all ages numbered 1,259, accounting for approximately 60 percent of the total population. Most of this imbalance resulted from a pronounced "excess" of men above eighteen years, in which age category they outnumbered women almost two to one. Although contemporary records do not supply many particulars, the social ramifications of the situation must have been great. Few of the newcomers took Indian wives, and prostitution was not openly countenanced. Even if one half of the girls between twelve and eighteen years had been considered to be of marriageable age—which they were not—42 percent of all adult males in Oregon were forced by demographic exigencies to remain single. Neither would the immigrations of the next several years ameliorate the problem.

As the population grew and alternative routes were established across the south flank of Mount Hood and southern Oregon, counting the annual influx became increasingly difficult. No longer could one individual witness an entire immigration and estimate its size with certainty. Roughly two thousand persons came in 1845 and about half that number the next year.

Approximately five thousand persons crossed overland land to the Pacific in 1847. Perhaps two-thirds of these went to Oregon, most of them to the valleys south of the Columbia River. Settlement of the long-standing jurisdictional dispute between Great Britain and the United States in the latter's favor, combined with the unsettled state of affairs in California, caused many to avoid the southern country. Then, too, the federal government was expected to pass soon a donation land act providing free land for Oregon immigrants.

In many respects 1847 may be regarded as the decade's last "normal" year of migration. Destruction of the Whitman Mission, and resulting Indian hostilities east of the Cascades, combined with the discovery of gold in California to alter dramatically the direction and scale of westward

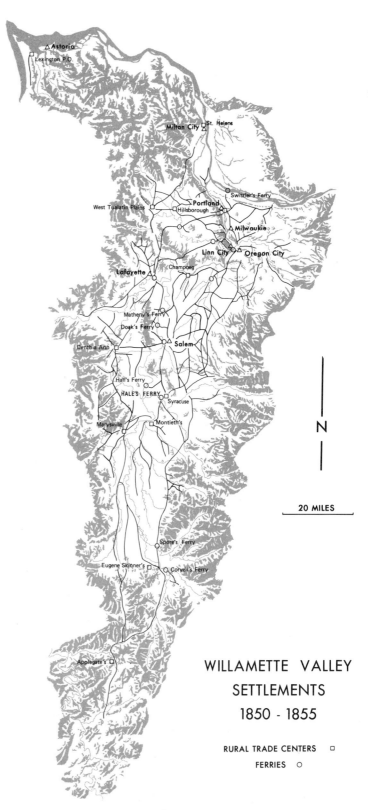

WILLAMETTE VALLEY
SETTLEMENTS
1850 - 1855

RURAL TRADE CENTERS □
FERRIES ○

MAP 4

TABLE 1
CENSUS OF OREGON, 1845

	No. of House-keepers	No. of Heads of Families	Under 12 Yrs. of Age		12 and under 18 Yrs.		18 and under 45 Yrs.		45 and over		Whole Number		Total Popu-lation
			M[a]	F[a]	M	F	M	F	M	F	M	F	
Champoeg	18	57	69	54	12	15	136	53	15	7	234	129	361
Clackamas	24	85	142	136	45	37	171	114	42	18	400	305	705
Clatsop	17	29	14	18	1	3	42	8	4	1	61	30	91
Tualatin	14	127	115	109	28	24	142	90	26	6	309	229	538
Yamhill	16	109	79	65	31	24	124	57	23	9	257	158	415
Total	89	405	419	382	117	103	615	322	110	41	1259	851	2110

[a]M = males; F = females.

SOURCE: H. O. Lang, *History of the Willamette Valley* (Portland, 1885), 288.

TABLE 2
TERRITORIAL CENSUS: 1849

	Males under 21 Years	Males 21 Years and Older	Females of All Ages	Foreigners			Total Number of Citizens	Total Number of Foreigners	Total
				Males under 21 Years	Males 21 and over	Females of All Ages			
Benton	271	229	370				870		870
Clackamas	401	390	585		12	5	1,376	17	1,393
Tualatin (Washington)	346	293	468	4	23	8	1,107	35	1,142
Champoeg (Marion)	465	458	647	5	94	13	1,570	112	1,682
Clatsop	49	100	75		3		224	3	227
Linn	295	269	359				923		923
Polk	337	327	509		1		1,173	1	1,174
Yamhill	394	402	557	3	8	4	1,353	15	1.368
Total	2,558	2,468	3,570	12	141	30	8,606	183	8,779

movement. Countless thousands crossed the continent in the next several years, but relatively few favored Oregon over the mines of its southern neighbor. Even within the frontier settlements the primacy of the annual migration in the lives of the inhabitants gave way to events occurring in the south. In 1848 and 1849, uncounted hundreds left Oregon in search of fortune. Some authorities put the number at about two thousand for 1848 alone.

Although many fortune seekers returned after a season or two, a great number did not. This is attested to by the hundreds of names listed on the rolls of early emigrant trains that do not appear in later censuses. Whether we accept estimates of 700 or 1,400 persons for the 1848 immigration, Oregon for at least one year probably experienced a net decline in population. Logically, it might appear that attrition should have been greatest among the unmarried men who had few personal attachments and social responsibilities at home. The special territorial census ordered by Governor Joseph Lane prior to the arrival of the 1849 immigration proves, however, that such was not the case. Of the 8,779 persons enumerated south of the Columbia River, 5,121, or fully 59 percent, were males, a proportion virtually unchanged from four years previously (table 2).

The rush of other events in 1848 and 1849, and the attendant diversion of public interest, led contemporary observers and later chroniclers to pass lightly over the immigrations of these years. Estimates vary so greatly for 1848 that all are extremely suspect. For the 1849 immigration, the data are at best only inferential. In the interval between the territorial census of 1849 and the federal census of 1850, the official population of Oregon south of the Columbia grew from 8,779 to 11,873 persons, an increase of 3,094. At least 270 of these may be accounted for by natural increase. The remaining 2,824 cannot be definitely assigned to returning miners or to either the 1849 or 1850 migrations. Contributing to the uncertainty is the fact that the federal enumeration of the latter year was conducted in the various counties at different times between September 1850 and March 1851. If there was truth in claims published in the Oregon Spectator that the 1850 immigrants were not counted, the matter might be easily decided. Detailed examination of the manuscript census, however, uncovers at least one identifiable group of about two hundred newcomers. The number of others who might have already disappeared into the fabric of society cannot be determined.

Adding to the indefinite estimates of yearly immigration was the changed character of the frontier's economic activity after the California Gold Rush. Demand in the mines for Oregon's agricultural surplus and lumber focused new attention on commerce and logging in the northern forests. Grain, which, except for the Alaskan trade, had been formerly consumed in local markets, was now grown for export. Financial considerations dictated that most of this new business should center on the Columbia River, and to serve the needs of farmer and sailor a series of small landings sprang up below the falls of the Willamette.

Prior to the discovery of gold several attempts had been made to usurp Oregon City's place by laying out alternative townsites, but none had been rewarded with success. As early as 1842, lots had been marked in Linn City on the west side of the Willamette's falls, and, in 1845, streets were surveyed downstream at Francis Pettygrove's Portland. With increased shipping on the river after 1848, new life was breathed into old schemes, for shoals and rapids in the Willamette River below the falls normally prevented large vessels from ascending the stream beyond Portland. Houses

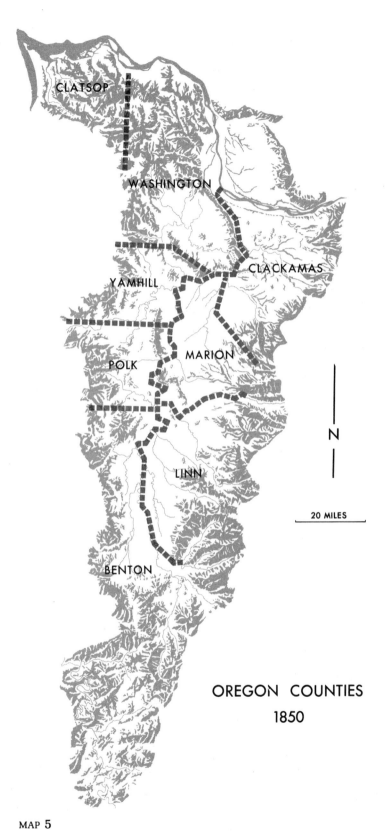

OREGON COUNTIES
1850

MAP 5

and wharves were constructed at forest clearings where speculators hoped the frontier's new metropolis would rise. St. Helens, Milton City, Milwaukie, and Portland vied with one another for the growing export trade by building primitive roads inland to the Tualatin Plains. Lumber mills were erected and work gangs were employed to cut timber and construct buildings. Upriver, Salem and several smaller hamlets served the rural districts of the interior. In two short years the number of townspeople more than doubled, so that by 1850, they included almost 25 percent of the entire population. Henceforth, there would be not one, but two frontiers in Oregon—one rural, the other urban (map 5).

CHAPTER 2

Motivation and Migration

DURING the fall and winter of 1850, some 11,873 persons lived in the settlements south of the Columbia River. Except for a few Indian women who had been taken as wives by white men, they were immigrants or children of immigrants, chiefly those who had arrived in the previous seven years. All were, to some degree, psychologically bound to one another by the shared experience of migration. For many, the long sea voyage or tedious overland journey which brought them to Oregon was the most important event of their lives, a dividing line between the past and the future. To deal with these people, and the communities they established, without considering this basic fact would ignore one of the most vital elements in the development of the frontier landscape.

Motive is fundamental to migration. Men do not abandon their homes and travel to new regions without reason. Motivation becomes an increasingly important factor the more distant the prospective country and the more difficult the journey. The two thousand miles to the Pacific Coast represented the longest single journey attempted by the American settler. Unlike the earlier, shorter migrations of the Atlantic seaboard or the Mississippi Valley, the pioneer, for the first time, was confronted by the unfamiliar environments of arid plains and formidable mountains. Retreat from this farthest frontier was all but impossible. Success depended upon careful planning and willingness to expend considerable effort. Prospective settlers had to accumulate information concerning route and destination. They had to sell farms and businesses, obtain wagons, livestock, food, and equipment, and organize a wagon train. All this, in turn, depended upon an unusually great incentive.

If motivation is a key to better understanding the migration, it is also a problem. Few aspects of the westward movement are more difficult to analyze. Diaries and reminiscences suggest that there was often no single overriding reason for leaving an established home for the distant frontier. Often there were at least several of equal importance, and these were so interwoven as to be indistinguishable. Numerous inconsequential irritants could develop a feeling of general dissatisfaction which only needed some plausible excuse to initiate action. Probably many of the Oregon frontiersmen would have been hard pressed to explain their real motives at the time of their migration. Reasonable explanations would be offered in later years for what may have been at the time an essentially irrational act.

A recurring theme of more than a century's Fourth of July oratory has been the political idealism of the immigrants and how their inspired nationalism drove them to wrest the land from the "fierce hold of the British lion." Contemporary manuscripts and private reminiscences indicate, however, that political motives were of almost no importance to the bulk of the people. Statements to the contrary are found almost exclusively in the memoirs of old politicians who from force of habit later attributed their every action to patriotism. Peter H. Burnett, California's first state governor and Oregon pioneer of 1843, was at once both typical and more honest than most when he stated, "I went to Oregon for three purposes, (1) to assist in building up a great American community on the Pacific Coast, (2) to restore the health of Mrs. Burnett, (3) to become able to pay my debts."[1]

Even aspiring politicians had mercenary reasons for migrating. They had to, because for the most part they were responsible family men. Adventure, political or otherwise, was a luxury in which only single men could indulge. The costs of failure were too great, the avenues of escape from Oregon too uncertain for most men to risk their children's lives on patriotic slogans. To the large degree families dominated the annual migrations, motives were of a more substantive nature. In this regard one pioneer noted that "the fact is, this country—and it will surprise you a little if you are not aware of it—is settled by a very steady people, a plain people, and it was settled by families; a very moral people as a rule."[2]

Economic reasons were certainly the basis for early corporate ventures. Likewise, the profit motive undoubtedly stirred the emigrants from the western states who came after 1842. During the first several decades of the century, the aspirations of these people were satisfied with opportunities much closer at hand. Settlement of the vast Mississippi Valley had hardly begun, and the prices received for agricultural products were generally good. If a farm life did not appeal to an individual, there were the lead mines of Illinois, a multitude of possibilities in the growing cities, the Rocky Mountain fur companies, or perhaps even the overland trade between western Missouri and Mexico.

The Panic of 1837 undermined many of these options and years of economic uncertainty followed. Crop prices fell in response to depression and agricultural overproduction. As a result, farm mortages, contracted during years of advancing speculation, could not be paid.

Exacerbating the economic problems of that large segment of the population living in the river bottoms of Missouri, Iowa, and Illinois were a succession of high waters that occurred in 1836, 1844, and 1849. The flood of 1844 was especially destructive, exceeding all previous records. The entire width of the Missouri River Valley between the bluffs was inundated. Hundreds of farms disappeared into the swirling waters. Loutre Island was devastated, and Franklin, Missouri, the original terminus of the Santa Fe Trail, was swept away. If that was not enough, the receding waters brought a sickness that prevailed throughout the country.

Men sought alternatives and in their search some grasped the almost illusory promises of distant places, countries remote from the all too real problems of the work-a-day world. Being members of an essentially agrarian society that attached great value to ownership of real estate, many automatically translated their quest into one for cheap or free land in the Far West. In this they were encouraged by the activities of a varied assortment of publicists and politicians who from 1820 onward had championed the twin causes of American settlement and free land in Oregon.

When the first large parties trekked overland to the Columbia River in 1843, positive political support for free land appeared imminent. The pioneers did not realize that Congress would wait eight long years before suitably rewarding them. Events proved that the inactivity of the federal government did not impede rural settlement. To the contrary, it allowed early settlers in the absence of legitimate national authority to assume complete autonomy and create their own land policy. In the spring of 1843, the American community in the Willamette Valley formed an independent, provisional government to maintain public order and protect the rights of individuals, particularly the right to preempt and hold unclaimed real estate without cost.

Promises of economic betterment and the concomitant opportunity to obtain free land were undoubtedly vital factors affecting the motivation of Oregon immigrants. Retrospective views and economic studies notwithstanding, many believed they would be richer for the journey. Even so, few ever admitted to being influenced solely by financial considerations.

If pioneer journals and reminiscences are interpreted literally, concern for physical health ranked at least as high, if not higher than, economics as an inducement to overland migration. Scores of contemporary observers lingered on the subject of sickness and disease throughout the great Mississippi Valley and the attendant pursuit of health that led families ever farther westward. Unlike the economic background to migration, this second search has received little attention. Later flights of health seekers into California and the Southwest, although more thoroughly documented, have been usually considered aberrations somehow outside the mainstream of western settlement history. Such was certainly not the case in early Oregon, where immigrants ranked health among the most important reasons for moving west.

Those of us born into a medically advanced society may find it difficult to fully comprehend the depth of such concern and the conditions that spawned it. When we consider the problems faced by people on the frontier, we are inclined to think of Indian warfare, the conquest of natural environment, or the difficulties associated with establishing a viable economy. All these shrink to insignificance before the question of health, for, without the latter, all other accomplishments became more difficult or impossible. Whether situated in the coastal plantations of Jamestown and Plymouth in the seventeenth century, or in the expanses of the trans-Appalachian wilderness and Far West in later years, the pioneer always suffered from disease. Health, the most vital factor in the successful occupation of new lands, was also the one element over which men had the least control.

During the greater part of the colonial period, the dispersed, rural character of the American population and poor communications combined to check the spread of pestilence. Individual communities and occasionally entire regions suffered general infections. Instances of widespread contagion were, however, generally rare. This situation changed radically after the Revolution with the growth of cities and the construction of turnpikes, canals, and railroads. Rapid communication together with a more densely settled populace and poor sanitation created circumstances conducive to sickness, and throughout the nineteenth century a succession of terrifying epidemics of almost every conceivable type struck the nation.

The people of the trans-Appalachian West were especially affected, for besides such long familiar diseases as measles, mumps, scarlet fever, whooping cough, dysentery, and smallpox they now faced a host of unknown fevers and influenzas endemic to the region. The depressing lists of contagions found in the lowlands during the first half of the century read almost as a lexicon of sickness.

Scarlet fever, a long established killer, struck Kentucky and Ohio country in 1791 and 1793, and from 1821 onward was found every year somewhere in the greater Mississippi River basin. In 1807, 1815–16, and 1824–26, great pandemics of influenza swept through the upper Mississippi and Ohio river valleys, and, in 1813–14 and 1843, respectively, widespread outbreaks of this same disease occurred in Ohio's Western Reserve and along the lower Mississippi. In 1816, meningitis spread through Illinois and the surrounding territory. By 1830, measles was endemic, and in 1835–36 the population suffered from epidemic ophthalmia. Outbreaks of smallpox became so common as to be no longer especially noteworthy, and the occurence of erysipelas, or "black tongue," assumed epidemic proportions in 1843, 1844, and 1845. For sheer terror, however, no disease surpassed Asiatic cholera, which advanced throughout the western states in 1832, 1833, and 1834. In rapid succession, Detroit, Chicago, Indianapolis, St. Louis, Cincinnati, and New Orleans were devastated. Mortality in many places exceeded 20 percent.

Nearly as fearful to western farmers as cholera was the dreaded "milksickness," or "puking fever," of frontier settlements, an illness caused by eating the tainted milk or meat of animals poisoned by the white snakeroot, *Eupatorium ageratoides.* From the Yadkin and Chattahoochee rivers, westward throughout Kentucky and Tennessee and in southern Ohio, Indiana, Illinois, Iowa, and Missouri the sickness of man and livestock yearly forced many families to abandon their farms and move on to new districts. Whole communities were broken up and dispersed by mortality rates commonly as high as 25 percent. Unlike other terrors, milksickness was not a passing phenomenon that quickly ran its course and disappeared. As long as the poisonous plant was present in sufficient quantity, sickness and death continued.

Much more deadly than the passing epidemics was pulmonary tuberculosis. With the possible exception of malaria, this disease took more lives on the frontier than any other affliction. Yet, it was seldom mentioned with great anxiety in accounts of the day. Its symptoms were easily recognized, but the slow and progressive nature of the infection, and its lack of terrifying visual effects similar to cholera or smallpox, served to lessen public concern. Its contagious nature was not recognized, and so widespread was its occurrence that to contract it was considered as normal as growing old. Some idea of its inroads is gained by one military surgeon's reports from southeastern Missouri made during the 1860's: "In conducting medical examinations with a view to military service, I have found developed tuberculosis a cause of exemption in more cases than any other disease, the ratio being seventy-four in every thousand."[3] Considering the faulty diagnostic procedures of the day, actual infection may easily have been several times this figure.

Eighteen fifty was a cholera year, and the nation's press and overland diaries dwelt upon its terrible afflictions. Hardly anywhere was there more than a passing mention of tuberculosis—certainly it created no panic. Yet, data contained in the United States Census of Mortality for that year reveal that "consumption" was the disease most prominently featured in death figures. If the abnormally large number of cholera cases is ignored, tuberculosis accounted for approximately one death in every five resulting from sickness.

Ralph Geer, an early Oregon immigrant, later remembered that, "I came here for my health like thousands of others. I was living in Illinois and told my wife if Knox County was not good enough for me to live in I would die there. Some thought I was getting consumption."[4] Given the widespread occurrence and deadly effects of the malady, it is understandable that at least a few persons might seek relief in the Far West. The real wonder is perhaps that more did not come.

The disease that did cause mass migration was malaria, or, as it was then known, "fever and ague." Unlike consumption, this malady's active symptoms were immediately recognizable and extremely uncomfortable. The printed literature and correspondence of the period often commented on its widespread occurrence and injurious influence on society. Charles Dickens, Mark Twain, and other noted authors immortalized its scrawny, careworn victims. Travelers feared for their lives. Henry R. Schoolcraft wrote of his exploration of the Illinois River:

The appearance of the inhabitants has corresponded with the opinion before expressed of the unhealthiness of the country. Pale and emaciated countenances; females shivering with ague, or burning with intermittent fever unable to minister to their children; and every member of a numerous family suffering from the prevalent malady at the same time. . . . In this country life is at least fifty percent below par in the months of August and September. I have often thought that I ran as great a risk every season I spent here as I would in an ordinary battle. I really believe it seldom happens that a greater proportion of an army falls victim to the sword during a campaign, than there has of the inhabitants of Illinois to disease, during a season that I have been here.[5]

Malaria seems to have been one of the more formidable obstacles to rapid settlement of the trans-Appalachian West. Some medical experts of the period even doubted that much of the lowlands would ever prove habitable, and the experiences of many farmers supported their contention. Entire communities were abandoned along the Missouri, Illinois, and upper Mississippi rivers. All reports emphasize the ubiquity of malaria. In mitigated forms it occurred as far east on the Ohio River as Pittsburgh, northward on the Mississippi to Fort Snelling, Minnesota, and up the Missouri River beyond Fort Leavenworth. From the early years of the century until the 1870s, most of the population residing within this area was afflicted to some degree. Death was not uncommon, but even more serious was the partial debilitation of millions of survivors. Vitality was sapped from generations of children and adults already burdened by poor living conditions and a host of other infections. With reason, the idea prevailed during the early nineteenth century that some western states were graveyards. Many who were not carried off immediately were hastened to their deaths by the zealous purging and bleeding of inept physicians. Compounding the deleterious effects of common medical practice were the poor living conditions and sanitary practices of the pioneers. Their diet was often inadequate and their eating habits faulty. Malnutrition, gross obesity, and scurvy were found everywhere. The lower classes were often poorly clothed and crowded together in hovels where basic standards of cleanliness were ignored and severe drunkenness was common.

Since many people were weakened by the rigors of frontier life and had little resistence to infection, complications, such as pneumonia, often followed upon even inconsequential illnesses, and each winter many died. In this regard, it is interesting to note that while the terrible epidemics of the period excited wonder and became the subjects of innumerable popular and medical investigations, they were hardly ever mentioned by the early Oregon settlers. Evidently the immigrants felt that the "unhealthy climate" of the Mississippi Valley with its feverish summers and deadly winters was more deserving of comment. Winter was especially recognized as a primary factor behind the overland migration. In explaining his several reasons for emigrating from Western Missouri to Oregon, Peter Burnett stressed that "the health of Mrs. Burnett had been delicate for some three years and it was all we could do to keep her alive through the winter in that cold climate. Her physician said the trip would either kill or cure her."[6]

John Ball, enroute to Oregon with Nathaniel Wyeth, wrote of the Burnetts' neighborhood, "This is the upper part of the state of Missouri, and is considerably settled. It has excellent land, mostly prairie, and is inhabited by emigrants from Kentucky, Tennessee, and Virginia. They have many slaves. . . . There is not a sufficient supply of good water, nor should I think from the countenances of the people, that it was very healthy." Then he added prophetically, "the inhabitants of this region know more of the mountains and Santa Fe than of New York and New England."[7] Already the Missouri frontiersmen were becoming dissatisfied with their lot and were searching for new and better lands farther west. These were the people who would fill the ranks of the first major overland migrations to Oregon. Some wished to escape financial troubles. Others sought free land. The greatest number, however, would leave "mostly because of periodical malarial sickness."

CHAPTER 3

Sources of Information about the Oregon Frontier

INFORMATION, its acquisition, dissemination, and use, is central to the development of motives and is a prerequisite to any decision to migrate. Without knowledge, an informed choice between an existing situation and possibly better alternatives is impossible. Without knowledge, there can be little hope, little anticipation of change. Disease, economic depression, and social conflict create dissatisfaction, but it is only information that allows the translation of that uneasiness into movement.

Western exploration and the communication of resulting geographic knowledge were often slow, indefinite processes. On the trans-Mississippi frontier, they began in the seventeenth century with French efforts to establish economic domination over the continental interior and continued for more than a hundred years before America's acquisition of Louisiana. Hundreds of men journeyed into the wilderness, but few were literate and fewer still wrote of their travels. The record of exploration was essentially an oral one, and information so laboriously collected seldom enjoyed circulation beyond the small rural communities of the frontier. Just how much the faceless adventurers knew, and how much unacknowledged data they passed on to others, is today impossible to ascertain, but it is noteworthy that almost every major expedition mounted during the early American period incorporated within its ranks a few of their number.

After the departure of Lewis and Clark from St. Louis in 1804, explorers pushed forward into ever more distant lands. Official government surveys, merchants, and fur companies sent out literate men who returned to recount their experiences. Within several decades almost every important section of the Far West had been visited and described in print. Maps became less imaginative as the blank spaces were filled with new discoveries.

For those who were for some reason dissatisfied with their current situations this activity served to illuminate new alternatives. Men who had for years endured the deadly onslaught of malaria or tuberculosis as a matter of course were now told their sufferings need not continue. Debtors found new avenues of escape. Increasingly, the blandishments of distant lands caught the attention of the American public, and as substantive information destroyed the fearful mysteries of the unknown, some people even began to move.

Prospective emigrants had three primary sources of information upon which they could draw. Best known, and most widely circulated, were such popular books as Hall J. Kelley's *Geographical Sketch of That Part of North America Called Oregon* (1830), John Wyeth's *Oregon, or a Short History of a Long Journey from Atlantic to Pacific* (1833), Washington Irving's *Astoria* (1836), Thomas Farnham's *History of Oregon Territory* (1844), Daniel Lee and J. H. Frost's *Ten Years in Oregon* (1844), and Langford Hasting's *Emigrant's Guide to Oregon and California* (1845).

Another source of information readily available in the more settled sections of the western states was the press. In many respects newspapers were more informative and more influential than books. They were cheaper, the news was current, and contributors were numerous and experienced. As western travel became increasingly common, so did reports of it in the press. The activities of fur companies, government expeditions, Santa Fe merchants, tourists, and finally emigrants were almost daily fare for publishers.

Papers such as *Weekly Reveille* (St. Louis), *Liberty Tribune* (Liberty, Missouri), *Western Expositor* (Independence), and *The Gazette* (St. Joseph) educated the readers of their districts in the geography and history of the West. Especially popular, in later years, was the publication of public or private letters and interviews. On rare occasions, these were of general interest and were widely published. More often, circulation reached only into the adjoining counties. Generally, each district had its own letter writers drawn from the ranks of its former citizens.

Public lectures were the third formal method of educating Americans to the possibilities offered by the new frontiers. Upon his return to the United States from the Pacific Northwest in 1838, Jason Lee stimulated widespread interest in Oregon by speaking in more than eighty cities and towns throughout the East. Likewise Marcus Whitman created something of a sensation with his descriptions of Oregon. Daniel Waldo and many others from the malarial western counties of Missouri were particularly impressed with his orations concerning the healthfulness of the Oregon climate.

Besides the famous publicists there were dozens of lesser known, but more effective, recruiters. Almost always, these were men who had returned to old residences to convince their families and neighbors to move. These speakers' long-standing membership in local communities gave their comments a greater credibility than that enjoyed by the New England missionaries and other outsiders. A typical case was Albert Davidson, eldest son of one of Burlington, Iowa's first settlers. He returned from Oregon in 1846 and "gave such a splendid account of the country; in fact made a number of speeches in Illinois, Iowa, and Missouri and there was a very large immigration came out on that account."[1]

Books, newspapers, and lectures were the three public media by which information was spread throughout the western states. Because of their relatively great circulation, and the fact that printed materials have survived the ravages of time better than other records, it has been easy to attribute greater influence to these forms of communication than they perhaps deserve. Despite all of his lectures and published writings, Jason Lee directly influenced only several dozen persons to move to Oregon.

Pioneer manuscripts indicate that most persons considered outsiders and the media to be only secondary sources of information that required confirmation by more trustworthy material. Newspapers contained conflicting reports as to the desirability of various routes and destinations. Fact and fancy were indistinguishable—a serious defect when reliable information was absolutely necessary for survival. The journey to Oregon was too dangerous, and the northwest frontier too wild and distant for a man to risk the lives of his family merely on the public statements of complete strangers whose motives and experiences were unknown.

The only manner in which information could be adequately substantiated was through private connections—either by first-hand experience or by personal familiarity with an unimpeachable source. Although such advisement provided the surest knowledge, it could not, by its very nature, become an avenue of widespread communication. Any given "explorer" knew only a limited number of people who would believe implicitly whatever he said. His statements might qualify as indisputable fact in his own family and neighborhood, but in the next county they would be interpreted as hearsay until checked against another personal account.

Reliance on individual contacts combined with primitive communications meant that intelligence, so laboriously collected, seldom enjoyed wide circulation or acceptance. Neighborhoods that sent many men into the wilderness knew a great deal about western geography. Those that did not, knew much less.

The implications of word-of-mouth communication were far reaching. For the members of a particular family or neighborhood the system meant that the choice of migration routes and eventual destination was in some degree restricted to those areas with which their close acquaintances were familiar. This in turn created a tendency for existing groups to migrate as units and to maintain themselves as more or less spatially definable bodies in new lands.

The details of individual cases varied, but the intensely personal character of the exchange of information was almost universal. The lines of communication were fantastically complex, interlocking associations of families bound together by intimate social relationships and blood. Together, these clans settled first Kentucky and Tennessee and then southern Indiana, the Illinois River Country, southern Iowa, and Missouri. Their men traveled throughout the West. They also fought together in the War of 1812, the Blackhawk War, and the Mormon Wars of western Missouri.

A fair sample of this social stratum was the Zumwalt clan which gained fame in the Indian Wars of the trans-Appalachian West. Adam Zumwalt moved to Lexington, Kentucky in 1781 and joined the local militia company. There he became well acquainted with Daniel Boone and many of his famous associates. Adam and his brother, however, were soon attracted to lands farther west, and they moved to that portion of New Spain now located within St. Charles County, Missouri. They were farmers and also distillers of whiskey that they sold to the Indians. Their incomes were modest, but their families were not. Adam had eight children, his son Solomon, fourteen.

Solomon later wrote that "brother Andrew started to oregon in the spring of 46. We still coruspondid. He first rote unfavrabel of the country. Then after staing in it a fiew yers he wrote very flatrin letors. He was a man that i cold depend on. So got in a notion to sel and moov to that far of country." Evidently he was not alone in his intention to cross the continent, for by 1850 there were forty-one Zumwalts located in eight Oregon households.[2]

Clan-based, intracommunity communication was influential not only in the accumulation and dissemination of information, but also in the formation of the wagon trains themselves. Contrary to the popular myth of courageous individuals, muster rolls of many overland parties indicate that nuclear families and single men often formed the minority. Just as confirmation of public information by reliable personal sources tended to protect the prospective emigrant from making fatal errors, strong ties between families in a train assured each a greater degree of protection in case of serious accident. Typically, the separate wagons were organized into messes based upon old neighborhood or kinship affiliations. Joel Palmer noted that, when he crossed the Plains in 1845, "every family had its own fixtures; but we called them messes because there were four or five wagons generally from the same neighborhood, or they were relatives and they assisted each other."[3]

The need for vouchsafed information, dependable assistance on the trail, and trustworthy aid in establishing a new home in the wilderness created a situation in which the clan operated more effectively than most other social units. These groups often formed the essential core of the overland migrations. Attached to them, for security, were many other unrelated individuals whose presence tended to confuse group identities. Nevertheless, contemporary observers recognized that the migration was overwhelmingly dominated by a class of people with remarkably similar regional and cultural backgrounds.

William Strong, an educated Vermonter and federal appointee to the Oregon Territorial Courts, was immediately impressed by the clear dominance of the Willamette Valley in 1850 by people "from Missouri and the western border of the western states. There were occasionally a few Yankees that came out here, but the great bulk of the settlements made by the emigrants were of the western element. They were a very honest class. . . . and not very fond of work. . . . they cared very little about luxuries; were very independent, and their lives were generally very good."[4]

Given the westerners' motivations and their greater accessibility to pertinent information and clan support, such a comment is not at all surprising. Analysis of "place of origin" data, contained within the manuscript schedules of the Seventh United States Census, indicates that significant differences existed in the contributions made by various regions and states to the Oregon population (table 3).

The western border states of Arkansas, Iowa, and Missouri formed the single most important region of origin, accounting for almost 23 percent of Oregon's total population. Missouri was especially prominent, 2,196 Oregonians having been born there—more than in any other state.

East of the Mississippi and north of the Ohio, three states combined to account for over 21 percent of Oregon's total population. Illinois was the most important with 993 persons, followed by Ohio with 836, and Indiana with 697. As might be expected of new frontier areas, the northern tier of Great Lakes states, Michigan and Wisconsin, sent very few individuals to the Pacific Northwest.

Persons born in the South Central states were also common south of the Columbia, representing slightly more than 9 percent of the frontier's population. Kentucky ranked fourth among all states sending emigrants west, while Tennessee, further south, ranked tenth.

In 1850 approximately two-thirds of all Americans resided in the Atlantic and Gulf states. It is noteworthy, therefore, that less than 19 percent of Oregon's population came from the long-settled coastal margins of the nation. The limited contribution of the Deep South is particularly striking. Fewer than eighty persons listed in the 1850 census were born between the Rio Grande and Savannah rivers. By any measure, the people of this region were outside the mainstream of migration to the Pacific Northwest. Moving northward

TABLE 3
Oregon Population by Place of Origin, 1850

Origin	Total	Percent of Oregon Population	Ratio of Males to Females
New England	493	4.16	
Connecticut	66	.56	3.57
Maine	105	.88	3.04
Massachusetts	176	1.48	3.73
New Hampshire	41	.35	7.20
Rhode Island	33	.11	5.50
Vermont	92	.78	2.65
Middle Atlantic	903	7.61	
Delaware	18	.15	2.60
New Jersey	65	.55	1.41
New York	532	4.48	3.58
Pennsylvania	288	2.43	2.74
South Atlantic	762	6.44	
District of Columbia	9	.08	3.50
Florida	3	.03	
Georgia	25	.22	2.14
Maryland	71	.60	3.18
North Carolina	164	1.38	1.98
South Carolina	33	.28	1.54
Virginia	457	3.85	1.90
Gulf	50	.37	
Alabama	18	.15	1.57
Louisiana	5	.04	
Mississippi	7	.06	1.50
Texas	20	.12	1.00
South Central	1091	9.19	
Kentucky	709	5.97	1.55
Tennessee	382	3.22	1.73
North Central	2587	21.79	
Indiana	697	5.87	1.31
Illinois	993	8.36	1.15
Michigan	45	.38	2.07
Ohio	836	7.04	1.79
Wisconsin	16	.14	1.00
Western Border	2685	22.62	
Arkansas	64	.54	1.06
Iowa	425	3.58	1.09
Missouri	2196	18.50	1.24
Far West	2249	18.94	
California	25	.21	.47
Oregon	2191	18.45	.99
Plains and Mountains	33	.28	1.36
Canada	261	2.20	2.94
Foreign Born (excluding Canada)	449	3.78	2.80
Unidentified	352	3.25	
Total	11,873	100.00	

along the Atlantic coast, representation increased again. From a mere three persons born in Florida, state totals steadily grew to 457 in Virginia. Among the Middle Atlantic states, New York and Pennsylvania were relatively prominent contributors, while the small coastal states were less so. Fewer still were people born in the Northeast. Despite the early familiarity of its merchants with the Northwest Coast and the preeminence of its missionaries in the affairs of the Willamette Valley, New England accounted for only slightly more than 4 percent of Oregon's 1850 population. Canadians were more numerous than persons from Massachusetts or Maine.

The foreign born formed a relatively insignificant minority on the Oregon frontier. Excluding Canadians because of their long-standing role in the exploration and settlement of the area, aliens numbered only 449, that is slightly less than 4 percent of the total. More than 90 percent of these came from just four countries; England and its smaller islands accounted for 166 persons, Ireland for 107, Scotland for 67, and Germany for 75.

The clear dominance of Oregon's population in 1850 by people from the Middle West is portrayed graphically by map 6. Information pertaining to state of birth has been combined with age and sex characteristics from the manuscript census schedules to indicate the basic demographic composition of each group. Absolute values have been used in the construction of the population pyramids so that the relative significance of any state or particular age-sex group can be easily estimated and compared.

As may be seen, state groups varied not only in size, but also in character. Especially evident are variations in sex composition among the emigrants from different regions. The skewing in favor of men is not at all unexpected, for migration was typically a process that favored young, adult males. In nineteenth-century American society, many strictures on the behavior and mobility of women were rigidly enforced. Unlike men, most women were quite literally bound to their families and enjoyed little choice in their place of residence.

The restricted movement of women is most evident in those elements of the population born farthest from the Oregon frontier. Comparison of the sexes shows that the ratio of men to women emigrants from the Northeast was extremely high, usually in excess of three to one. Imbalance was greatest between the ages of twenty and forty years.

Between the ages of twenty-five and thirty, for instance, there were more than six times as many men as women from New York.

Along the southeastern seaboard, inequalities were significantly reduced within both total populations and individual age groups. The two largest contributors, Virginia and North Carolina, sent slightly less than two men for every woman. Still more evenly balanced were the ratios of states situated west of the Appalachian Mountains. This western equalization of sex ratios was in keeping with a general trend exhibited throughout the nation for emigrants from more recently settled states to be successively younger and more equally divided between the sexes.

Since most women of the period existed entirely within the social framework of the family, regional variations in the sex ratio indicate fairly accurately that portion of each state's emigrants which was incorporated within normal family structures upon initially leaving the place of birth. Oregon settlers who came from Atlantic seaboard states were typically adult males between the ages of twenty and forty years who left their home states unmarried. Only from Virginia did there occur any real movement of both men and women and, hence, families. In Tennessee, Kentucky, and Ohio the role of the family clan as an important social unit in the overland migration increased, and in the western states it was clearly dominant.

By inference, age characteristics of original-state populations also reveal something of the chronology of the family migrations within the Middle West. Unlike normal population pyramids, most of those on the map are markedly constricted in the younger categories, especially in older states. Using the more family-sensitive female populations, certain age groups may be identified with interstate movements. Kentucky, for example, sent few children to Oregon. Those who came from the state were born mainly between 1805 and 1830, with a slight peak about 1820. In more recently settled Indiana, the majority were born between 1820 and 1845, the largest concentration around 1830. Farther west in Illinois and Missouri, the key dates were between 1825 and 1845, with a maximum at the end of the period 1840–45. In frontier Iowa, the dominant cohorts were contained almost entirely within the years 1840–45.

Such a neat and orderly progression of birthdates from one state to the next suggests that a spatially definable, social continuum existed within Oregon's immigrant population, an inter-

AMERICAN POPULATION OF OREGON
Age—Sex Characteristics by State or Territory of Birth

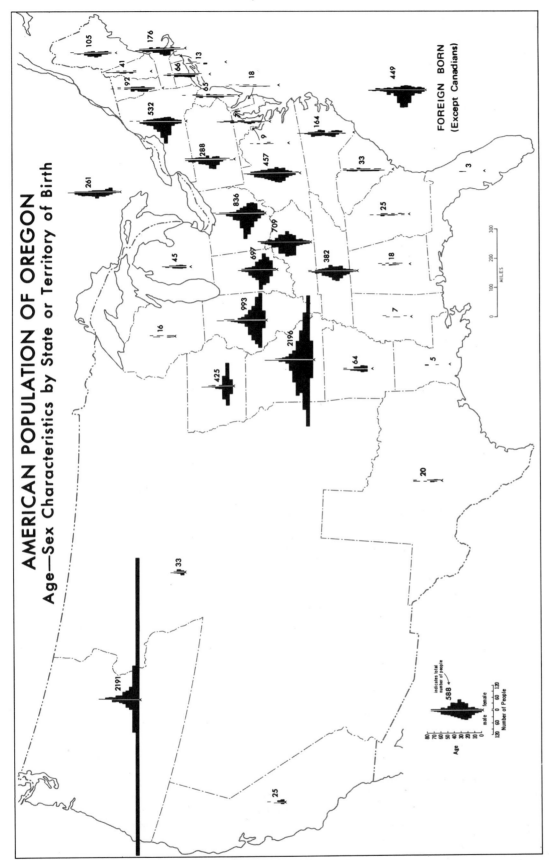

FOREIGN BORN
(Except Canadians)

MILES
0   100   200   300

indicates total
number of people
588

Age
80
70
60
50
40
30
20
10
0
120 60 0 60 120
male   female
Number of People

MAP 6

connection not adequately portrayed by the static display of map 6. In a society bound to the land, birthplace alone might suffice as an accurate indicator of cultural heritage, but in a dynamic, mobile society such as existed in the Middle West, the utility of charting birthplaces is greatly diminished. When attempting to characterize an individual's sectional affiliations and thereby possibly his cultural background, it may be as important to know his parents' origins and his own subsequent residences as it is to know his place of birth. The migrant's culture may be a product of any place he has lived.

Recognizing the necessity of somehow tracing the successive residences of the Oregon immigrants prior to their overland trek, the author devised a scheme whereby the movements of individuals could be at least partially inferred from the birthplaces of their relatives. Since the basic social unit of the period was the family, a complete survey was made of all normal households in Oregon to determine the relative importance and direction of family migrations eventually leading to the Pacific Northwest.

Normal families were defined for computational purposes as households of at least two persons with the same surname. Included were families having two parents and children and those in which a single adult of either sex resided with one or more children. Determination of family roles was based wholly on the age and sex of the individuals, the census having been sorted by household, name, and descending age. An age difference of at least eighteen years between the oldest male and the oldest "child" was required to identify a father-child relationship, a difference of at least fifteen years to establish a mother-child tie. In dwellings sheltering more than two generations, grandparents were considered to be the parents, and all other family members at least eighteen or fifteen years younger were grouped as children belonging to the same generation. In residences containing more than one household, each name group was treated as a separate normal family if it met the age-sex requirements. Married couples without children and groups of brothers and sisters without parents were excluded.

By applying this definition to the Oregon census of 1850, the author determined that 8,187 of the 11,873 persons enumerated south of the Columbia River were included in 1,456 family units. An example of one normal family was the Michael Shelly household, located between the Middle and Coast forks of the Willamette River in what was then Benton County. When enumerated in September 1850 it included:

TABLE 4

Name	Age	Sex	Birthplace
Michael Shelly	35	M	Kentucky
Lena Shelly	35	F	Tennessee
Henry Shelly	14	M	Illinois
Mary Shelly	11	F	Illinois
Ransom Shelly	9	M	Illinois
James Shelly	8	M	Iowa
Troy Shelly	5	F	Iowa
Roselle Shelly	4	F	Iowa
Ellen Shelly	1	F	Oregon

The basic method of analysis consisted of plotting the ordered sequence of related birthplaces found within each normal family to obtain a crude indication of the direction and magnitude of population flow. Households were first divided into two parts—parents and children. This was necessary to ensure that no confusion would result from erroneously computing nonexistent migration connections between the birthplaces of husbands and wives. For example, in the Michael Shelly home the parents were born in different states. From the data provided by the census it cannot be determined where Michael met and married his wife. It may have been in Kentucky, Tennessee, Illinois, or some other state. All that can be definitely said is that each had to migrate from his or her birthplace to Illinois, where their first surviving child was born. Hence, a trace was made from each parent to the eldest child and then through the other children in chronological order.

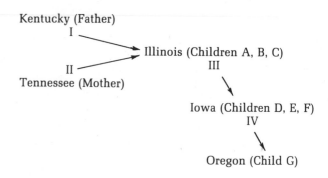

As the diagram indicates, there were four recognizable stages in the Shelly family's migratory history. The author made measurements at each of these thresholds, using two methods of computation. First, to determine the mass movement of population between states, a cumulative sum of individuals was calculated. That is, one person was counted moving across threshold I and another across threshold II. Across threshold III five persons were counted (two parents and three children), and across IV, eight. Since this procedure is heavily biased in favor of long-established or unusually fertile families, a second count was made using the family as the numeration unit. In this case one family was counted at each stage.

The author chose to measure the movement of families as well as the movement of individuals in order to resolve a fundamental question: how effectively raw population figures reflected the potential impact of settlers on the land. In Oregon each family was restricted to at most one square mile of ground. Whether a couple had ten children or two, their activities were constrained by the same acreage limitations. Hence, larger families did not necessarily possess more power to affect landscape change. It must also be remembered that parents, not small children, were the principal carriers of culture and technology, and there were only two parents in any family, no matter what its size.

One inherent defect of this method of analysis is the possibility of incomplete records. No way exists to determine from census schedules whether the family lived for a time in some state where no surviving child was born. Counterbalancing this difficulty, however, is the comprehensive nature of the census data and corroborating evidence gathered from other biographical and genealogical sources. The weight of this material suggests that, although some error exists in family records, the overview is more than sufficient to draw accurate conclusions about the directions and magnitudes of population movement to Oregon.

Because there existed a need for information pertaining to both the overall flow of emigrants from state to state and the movement of specific ethnic groups, the data were subjected to two methods of computation. For a panorama of the entire migration history of the population, a nonselective trace was first made on all individuals and families. The results are summarized in tables 5 and 6, each recording movements between forty-four states and nations.

By entering either array from the left or top margins, one can immediately determine the pre-cise amount and direction of any movement between two states. The author's original plans called for the use of this material in the construction of two comprehensive flow maps—one for individuals and another for families. The great number of origin-destination combinations, however, only promised uninterpretable confusion if mapped all together.

Even without graphic representation several general patterns may be recognized. In both tables it is evident that a handful of states dominated the migration history of Oregon's population. Missouri's overriding importance among the western states is underscored by the fact that 38 percent of all normal families (551) and 43 percent of all migrating individuals (2,865) passed through this single state. Illinois and Iowa ran a distant second and third with 1,115 and 814 persons respectively.

By studying the measured flow through these and other states, one can approximate the ethnic or sectional character of their transient populations. In the case of emigrants from Missouri, Illinois, and Iowa, for example, the relative importance of northern or southern people may be partially determined through computer traces and the maps derived from them (maps 7, 8, 9). In the Missouri-derived population, the most prominent contributing states were Kentucky (228), Indiana (228), and Illinois (209); followed by Tennessee (156), Ohio (137), and Virginia (115). Those emigrants from Kentucky, Tennessee, and Virginia may be reasonably assigned to a southern category, but the others are problematic, for in each of the states north of the Ohio River there were settlers from both the North and the South. The movement from Kentucky to Illinois accounted for the second largest influx of individuals to the latter state, and in Indiana there was at least a recognizable southern minority.

In contrast to Missouri, the populations derived from Illinois and Iowa drew a greater portion of their numbers from states north of the Ohio River. The five chief contributors of people to Illinois were Ohio (142), Kentucky (117), Indiana (104), New York (60), and Missouri (52). In Iowa, the major states represented were Illinois (171), Indiana (152), and Ohio (96). If population alone is considered, northerners appear to have clearly dominated the migration through both states. However, when an account is also made of family movement, the situation in Illinois changes markedly. Kentucky becomes the number one contrib-

TABLE 5

INDIVIDUAL MIGRATION

Origin	ALA	ARK	CAL	CON	DEL	FLA	GEO	HAW	ILL	IND	IOW	KY	LA	ME	MD	MAS	MIC	MIS	MO	NEB	NH	NJ
ALA		1													4				8			
ARK			1						8										34			
CAL																						
CON										1	2								4			
DEL										1					1				7			
FLA																						
GEO		1							1			4						4	8			
HAW																						
ILL		9	16							171	6								209	4		
IND		15							104		152	5					14		228			
IOW			4						26	13									54			
KY		1							117	49	20				4	1			228			
LA																						
ME			4					1		2	3								1			
MD									5	12		3							9			
MAS							6		4	3	9		6						5			
MIC									16	6	1								1			
MIS		1					5												1			
MO		10	13						52	6	37											
NEB																						
NH									7	3	1	1				2						
NJ									6	3	3				1			1	6			
NY		1	2					3	60	36	20	12					6		21			
NC	1	1					1		11	24	5	8							50			
OHI		3							142	94	96	18	5				13		137			
ORE			16						18	6		7							1			
PEN									42	33	7	1			1		4		15			6
SC		1					3		4	4		1							6			
TEN	1	16							33	18	11	3							156			
TEX																			12			
VT									8	6	2							2	4			1
VA									50	34	19	13			1			1	115			
WIS								1			5								4			
Austria																						
Australia																						
Belgium																						
Canada			1					1	10		2			1				9	1			
Chile																						
England	2								6		3	1							10			
France																						
Germany									1	3	1				7				5			
Ireland								1	4		3				2				2			
Scotland									5	1						5			2			
Pacific Islands																						

utor with eighty-seven families, and Ohio drops to second place with sixty-one. Taking the top eight contributing states, at least one half of the families moving to Illinois had southern antecedents, whereas only about 40 percent of the immigrant population (individuals) could be identified as coming from the South. The difference seems mainly due to a greater proportion of minors born north of the Ohio River. Many of these youngsters would have been normally counted as northerners, but were, in fact, children of southerners who had moved from Kentucky and Virginia during the early decades of the nineteenth century.

To more accurately determine the interstate migrations and regional importance of particular ethnic groups, the author segregated the data contained in tables 5 and 6 according to place of birth. Nine of the longer-settled eastern states

TABLE 5 (Continued)

Destination

Origin	NY	NC	OHI	ORE	PEN	SC	TEN	TEX	VT	VA	WIS	Austria	Australia	Belgium	Canada	Chile	England	France	Germany	Ireland	Scotland	Pacific Islands
ALA				6																		
ARK				71			5															
CAL				71																		
CON	3		9	9						2	1											
DEL			2	1																		
FLA																						
GEO			1	11																		
HAW				16																		
ILL			15	1115	5		4	10														
IND			32	373	6																4	
IOW			6	814						6	4											
KY	6	1	16	176	1		2	2		6												
LA				5																		
ME	1		1	25																		
MD			6	22	1		7													1		
MAS	5		5	23					5	1												1
MIC				50																		
MIS																						
MO			14	2865			6	9		4												
NEB				4																		
NH			3	3					1													
NJ	3		12	10	2										1							
NY			48	84	5				1	6	4				3							
NC			2	11		8				1												
OHI				312	9	1				4						1						
ORE			7		6										1							
PEN	5		40	23		1				12	1											
SC				2		3																
TEN			3	59						1												
TEX				27																		
VT	13		11	12	1										1	1						
VA	1		25	76	4		2								1							
WIS				15																		
Austria																						
Australia				28												11						
Belgium																						
Canada			12	148																		
Chile				7																		
England	1		3	31						1				18	13							
France			1																			
Germany			2	3																		
Ireland	5		13	4										3	4							
Scotland				7											1							
Pacific Islands				3																		

and Canada were identified as the "ethnic heart-lands"—that is, places from which most of the Oregon population ultimately derived its origin. Along the Atlantic Seaboard these were Maine, Massachusetts, New York, Pennsylvania, Virginia, and North Carolina. West of the Appalachian Mountains, Kentucky, Tennessee, and Ohio were included.

For each heartland, a filtered computer run was made that recorded only the movement of normal families having one or more births in the selected state. By design, there was only one count of a household's movement prior to the birth of an individual in the filter state, across the borders of the state of residence immediately preceding the filter state. Subsequent to the birth of a parent or child in the filter state all movements of the family were recorded. The result is a series of

TABLE 6
Family Migration

Origin	Destination																					
	ALA	ARK	CAL	CON	DEL	FLA	GEO	HAW	ILL	IND	IOW	KY	LA	ME	MD	MAS	MIC	MIS	MO	NEB	NH	NJ
ALA																						
ARK																						
CAL																						
CON																			1			
DEL																						
FLA																						
GEO												2										
HAW																						
ILL		1									13	2							16	1		
IND									8		11	3							21			
IOW										1									3			
KY		1							87	40	20				1	1			172			
LA																						
ME																			1			
MD									3			3							3			
MAS										1		1							1			
MIC																						
MIS																						
MO		1							7			1										
NEB																						
NH												1										
NJ									1													
NY									6		1	4										
NC		1							2	5	1	6							7			
OHI									6	9	6	4							13			
ORE			1									1										
PEN									1	1		1					1		1			
SC									2			1										
TEN									7	2	1	3							17			
TEX																			2			
VT																						
VA									6	4	3	13							13			
WIS										1												
Austria																						
Australia																						
Belgium																						
Canada										1												
Chile																						
England												1										
France																						
Germany									1													
Ireland																						
Scotland																			1			
Pacific Islands																						

traces, showing the origins and diffusion of Oregon's constituent population throughout the Mississippi Valley and their later convergence on the Pacific Northwest.

For a general impression of the flow from three key states, consult maps 10, 11, and 12. These require little description, for they are visually self-explanatory. A pattern of two distinct systems of flow north and south of the Ohio River emerges, and the amount of sectional mixing in Illinois, Iowa, and Missouri is clearly defined.

The computerized results proved useful for purposes other than the mapping of population movements. They allowed for the first time a detailed examination of the inherited sectional ties of persons born in and passing through the border states of the Middle West. Of the 2,865 individuals in normal households migrating from

TABLE 6 (Continued)

Origin	NY	NC	OHI	ORE	PEN	SC	TEN	TEX	VT	VA	WIS	Austria	Australia	Belgium	Canada	Chile	England	France	Germany	Ireland	Scotland	Pacific Islands
ALA				6																		
ARK				15			1															
CAL				14																		
CON	3		9	5					2	1												
DEL			2	1																		
FLA																						
GEO			1	2																		
HAW				5																		
ILL			2	228	2		1	2														
IND			7	119	1																1	
IOW			1	132					1	1												
KY	2	1	10	83	1		2	2		4												
LA				1																		
ME	1		1	10																		
MD			6	6	1	3														1		
MAS	5		5	14					5	1												1
MIC				10																		
MIS																						
MO			4	551			2	2		1												
NEB				1																		
NH			3	3				1														
NJ	3		8	3	2										1							
NY			32	60	3				1	4	4				3							
NC			2	11		8				1												
OHI				118	3		1			1								1				
ORE			1		1										1							
PEN	2		35	21			1			5	1											
SC				2		3																
TEN			3	35						1												
TEX				5																		
VT	5		8	10	1										1	1						
VA	1		22	45	1	2									1							
WIS				4																		
Austria																						
Australia				4												2						
Belgium																						
Canada			5	97																		
Chile				2																		
England	1		3	23						1				7	6							
France			1																			
Germany			2	3																		
Ireland	5		6	4										3	4							
Scotland				7											1							
Pacific Islands				1																		

Missouri to Oregon, 40 percent were connected by birth with persons born in Kentucky, 21 percent with Virginia, 16 percent with Ohio, and 8 percent with New York. Illinois's 1,115 emigrants were more evenly divided between northerners and southerners. Thirty-three percent were related to Ohioans, 31 percent to Kentuckians, 23 percent to New Yorkers, and 20 percent to Virginians. Although of mixed regional origins, Iowa's 814 emigrants were more northern in character. Thirty-eight percent can be linked to people from Ohio, 29 percent to Kentuckians, 18 percent to Virginians, and 15 percent to New Yorkers.

Filtered data also permitted a relatively exact determination of the total number of people, and families, exposed through kinship to the influence of specific state birth groups. Comparison of the numbers ultimately associated with each of the

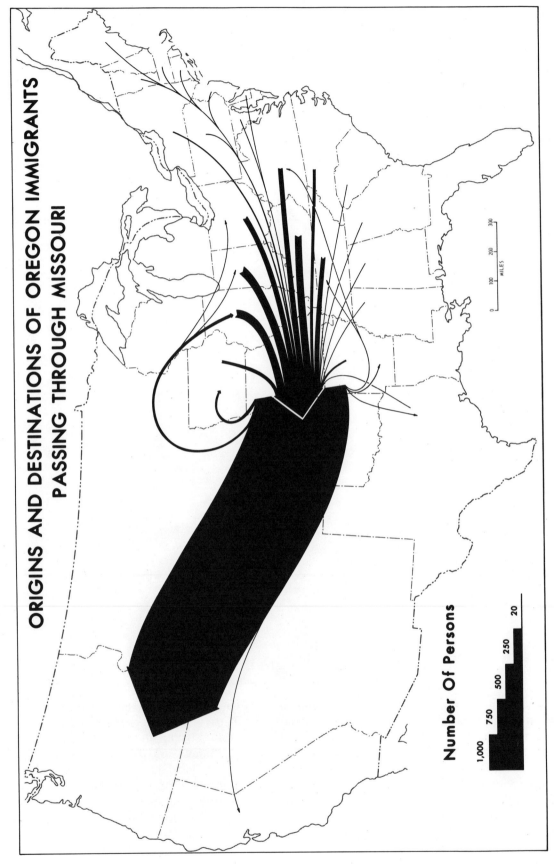

ORIGINS AND DESTINATIONS OF OREGON IMMIGRANTS PASSING THROUGH MISSOURI

Number Of Persons

1,000 750 500 250 20

MILES
0 100 200 300

MAP 7

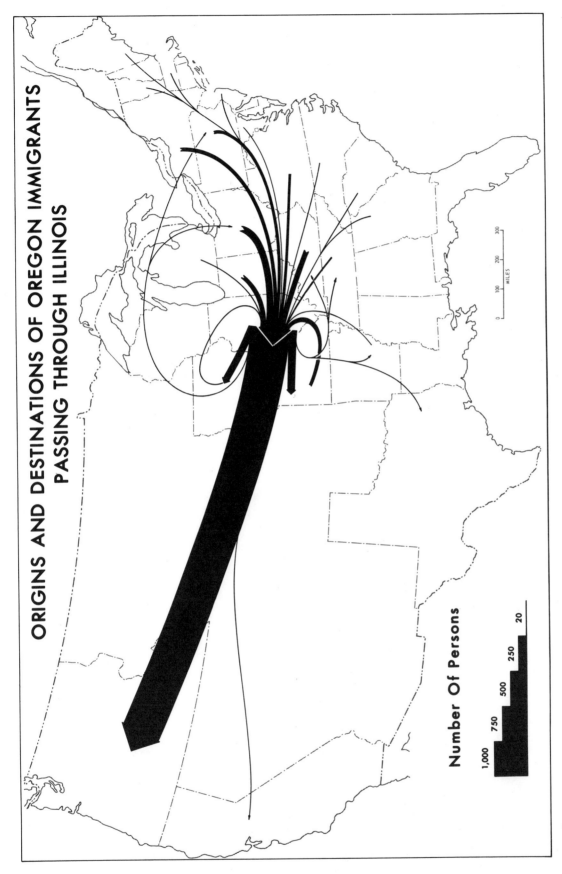

ORIGINS AND DESTINATIONS OF OREGON IMMIGRANTS
PASSING THROUGH ILLINOIS

Number Of Persons

1,000 750 500 250 20

MILES
0 100 200 300

MAP 8

ORIGINS AND DESTINATIONS OF OREGON IMMIGRANTS PASSING THROUGH IOWA

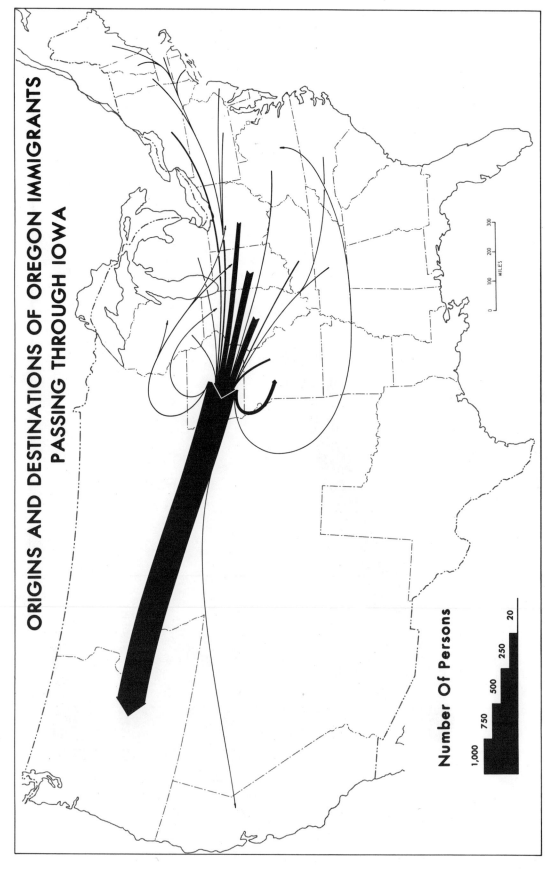

Number Of Persons

1,000
750
500
250
20

MILES
0   100   200   300

MAP 9

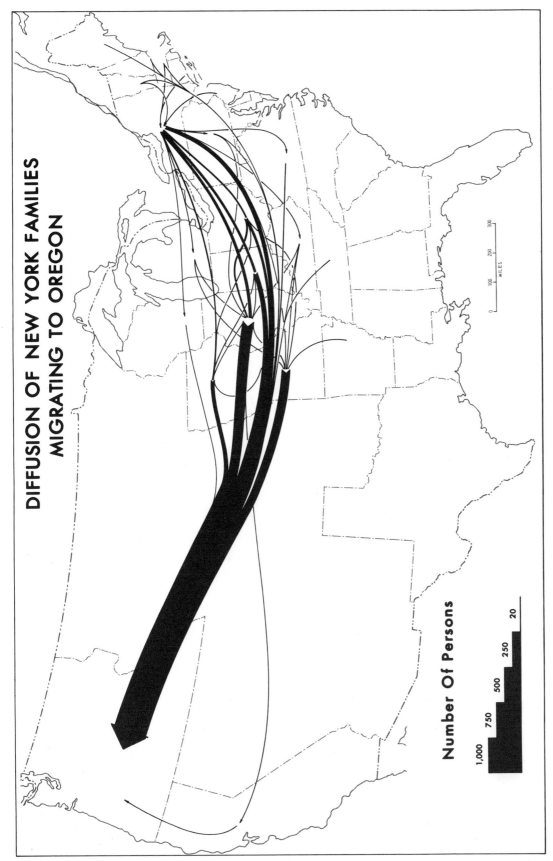

DIFFUSION OF NEW YORK FAMILIES
MIGRATING TO OREGON

Number Of Persons

1,000   750   500   250   20

0   100   200   300
MILES

MAP 10

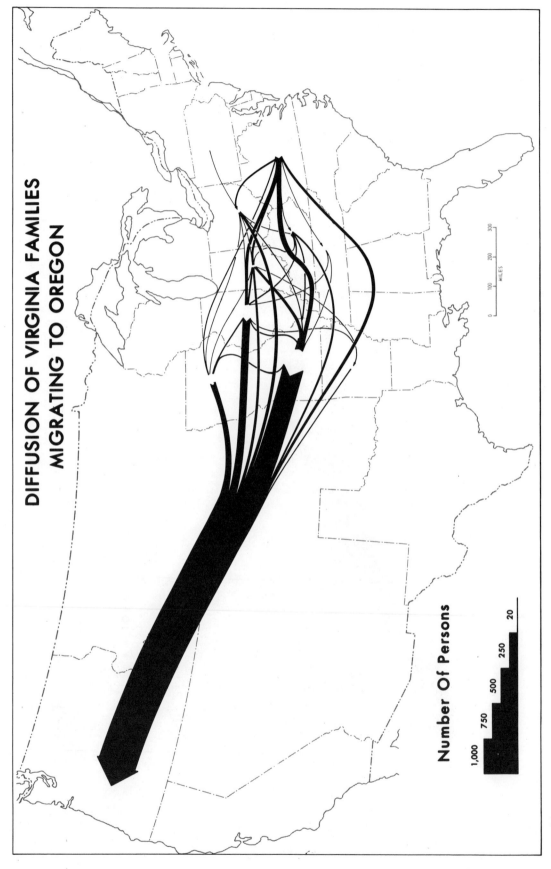

DIFFUSION OF VIRGINIA FAMILIES
MIGRATING TO OREGON

Number Of Persons

1,000
750
500
250
20

MILES
0 100 200 300

MAP 11

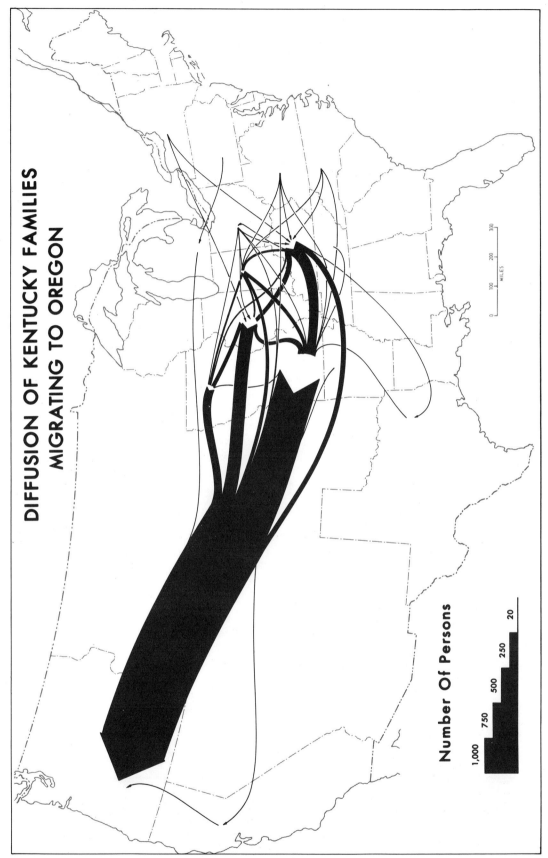

DIFFUSION OF KENTUCKY FAMILIES
MIGRATING TO OREGON

Number Of Persons

1,000   750   500   250   20

0   100   200   300
MILES

MAP 12

ten heartlands shows a very different ordering of importance than might have been assumed from the raw population data (table 7).

Although in terms of population they ranked second to Ohioans in Oregon, Kentuckians were found in more frontier homes and were related to more persons born outside their home state than any of the other eight states or Canada. Fully 24 percent of Oregon's normal households, containing 26 percent of the traceable population, had direct kinship ties with immigrants born in Kentucky. In every case where two states—one northern and the other southern—contributed similar numbers of immigrants, the southern state with its more extensive family ties and larger related population possessed a greater potential for cultural ascendancy. Virginia's and Tennessee's influence groups were both larger than New York's, and North Carolina's was more than twice as large as that of Massachusetts.

Census materials may be used to map the broad outlines of migratory flow, but they do not define successive places of residence more precisely than by state. Knowing the settlement histories of the states involved, more specific localities might be inferred, but such an approach is at best very indefinite. The possibility of error is great, and there is no certain method of determining the existence of clans.

Besides the census, one other source of locational data pertaining to the Oregon pioneers exists. This is the records of the Oregon Donation Land Claims, in which the county and state of each applicant's birth and marriage are noted. Strictly speaking, these documents do not correspond with the census, for they include only rural land claimants, and they reflect settlement to December 1, 1855. Rather than abstract only those applications for claims made prior to 1851, however, all were included in this study to provide an updated view of the origins of the settlers. This meant that absolute figures were larger than they would have been otherwise, but cross-checking indicated that the relative importance of different regions shifted only slightly during the five-year interim. Since birthplace alone is a poor indicator of cultural heritage in a relatively young migratory population, it was combined with place of marriage, and the two points were plotted on a single map (map 13).

The resulting sheet shows a striking localization of life's major events in the several major sections of the United States. In the heavily populated Northeast, few births or marriages were recorded except in upstate New York, where modest concentrations existed along the lower course of the Mohawk River and along the route of the Erie Canal from Rome to Buffalo. The great urban centers contributed almost no one to Oregon's rural population. The New York City and County group accounted for three entries and Boston for three more. For all practical purposes there was no crossing of urban-rural cultural boundaries. Overland migration was essentially from city to city or from farm to farm.

The minor role of the great coastal plain extending southward from New York along the Atlantic Seaboard and the Gulf of Mexico, is just as noteworthy as the insignificance of the eastern cities. Except for a few scattered cases near the shores of Delaware and Chesapeake bays, hardly an Oregon claimant was born or married within the region. Those who had resided in the coastal states lived almost entirely in the rolling country above the fall line or in the mountains and valleys beyond. East of the Blue Ridge, cases were widely distributed over the Piedmont with a slight concentration along the Potomac River. Only two counties listed more than ten births or marriages. These were Bedford County, Virginia, just east of the Blue Ridge, and Orange County, North Carolina, in the headwaters of the Neuse River above an elevation of eight hundred feet. Further south in South Carolina, Georgia, and Alabama every birth or marriage took place in the uplands.

The distribution of births and marriages in the hills of southwestern Virginia and eastern Tennessee was much more localized that that on the

TABLE 7
Relative Importance of Heartlands
as Reflected in Kinship Ties

Heartland	Total Persons in Oregon	Number of Related Persons	Number of Related Families
Ohio	836	1,794	304
Kentucky	709	2,191	355
New York	532	949	176
Virginia	457	1,186	199
Tennessee	382	1,116	175
Pennsylvania	288	716	119
Massachusetts	176	240	45
North Carolina	164	594	98
Maine	105	84	17
Canada	261	613	111

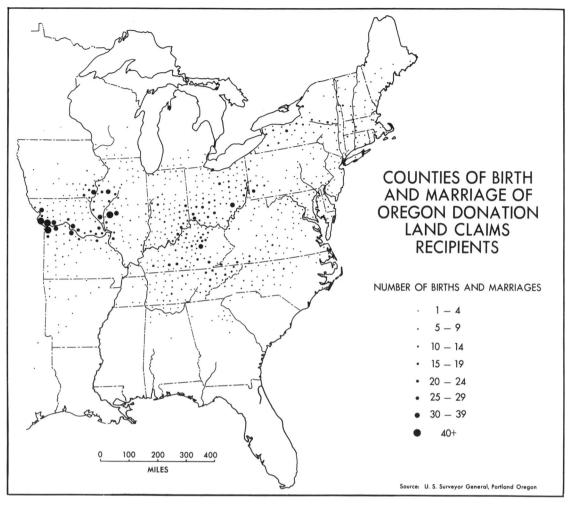

COUNTIES OF BIRTH
AND MARRIAGE OF
OREGON DONATION
LAND CLAIMS
RECIPIENTS

NUMBER OF BIRTHS AND MARRIAGES

·   1 — 4
·   5 — 9
·   10 — 14
·   15 — 19
·   20 — 24
·   25 — 29
·   30 — 39
●   40+

0   100   200   300   400
MILES

Source: U. S. Surveyor General, Portland Oregon

MAP 13

Piedmont. Many Oregon men came from the valleys lying between Cumberland Mountain and the Blue Ridge. The bulk of the Tennessee emigrants were mountaineers who came from districts further south along the tributaries of the Little Tennessee, Powell, and Holston rivers.

Although some local concentrations existed in the dissected Appalachian Plateau, the greatest number of cases in the Upper South occurred beyond the mountains, in the broad triangle formed by the Ohio and Tennessee rivers. The most important center was the bluegrass region of north central Kentucky around old Fort Harrod and Fort Boonesborough. Records show an area of general dispersion further south and west extending southward to the Tennessee River. Only along the northern edge of the Pennyroyal, between Hopkinsville and Glasgow, however, were there counties with more than fifteen instances of birth or marriage.

North of the Ohio, men from both North and South intermingled in the valleys of the Muskingum, Scioto, Little Miami, and Miami. Generally, Oregon immigrants came from the glaciated till plains of central and southwestern Ohio and southeastern Indiana. In the less well-drained northerly sections, the number of cases decreased. Likewise, relatively few were recorded along the Ohio River. In both areas the absence may have been related to flooding and attendant malaria. One modest concentration of entries came from the upper Ohio near Wheeling. Another occcurred at Cincinnati and a third in the counties across the river from Louisville, Kentucky. Further downstream towards the Mississippi "fever and ague" became increasingly virulent, and, except along the Wabash River, births and marriages of Oregon immigrants almost entirely disappeared.

Although most of the counties fell within the described pattern, there were several anomalous situations. The most striking was Morgan County, Ohio, which accounted for more births and marriages of donation land claimants than any other in that state. Contrary to the norm, Morgan County was situated about fifteen miles from the Ohio River in the dissected hill lands of the southeast. Neighboring counties such as Perry or Noble contributed few immigrants. A check of the county's thirty-three applications shows that most of the Morgan County families came overland relatively late. By 1850 only six had reached the Willamette Valley, the rest arriving during the next three years.

Although these people appear to have been predominantly of northern stock, their movement and occupation of land seem little different from those who preceded them. As among earlier arrivals, clan ties were of paramount importance in ensuring a successful migration and settlement. This is reflected by a distinct clustering of sixteen Morgan County families within twelve miles of one another between the South Fork of the Santiam and Calapooya rivers. Another smaller concentration of one-half dozen farms was located east of the Pudding River near Butte Creek.

West of the Wabash River, the prairies of central Illinois interposed to retard settlement. Births and marriages occurred in significant numbers only along the Mississippi River. Upstream from the mouth of the Ohio, the first important district was located around Cahokia, across the river from St. Louis, Missouri. More imposing concentrations lay on either side of the Illinois River in counties settled early by woodland farmers from the Upper South. A westward extension of this northern cluster included southeastern Iowa.

As has already been noted, Missouri was the largest contributor of immigrants to Oregon. Admittedly, most of these were children, but the broad range of ages in many families indicates that their terms of residence in the state were not necessarily brief. American occupation was already well underway by 1810, and persons born in the state had often reached their majority before crossing the plains. During the early decades of the century, the primary axis of travel and settlement lay along the Missouri River. In the river bottoms and the backcountry on either side, men from Kentucky and Tennessee opened farms and established such famous early towns as Franklin, Liberty, and Independence.

Because of their early settlement and their participation in the activities of the Santa Fe trade and the fur companies, the inhabitants of the Missouri River districts were among the most numerous of the emigrant groups. Records of births and marriages were especially common along the left bank between the Booneslick settlements and St. Charles County. Still further upstream was situated the state's bustling western frontier. There eight counties contained the centers of trade and rural settlement, and each of these sent large numbers of emigrants to Oregon. Combined they formed by far the greatest source region of Oregon immigrants in the entire United States.

CHAPTER 4

The Localization of Settlement in Oregon

THE PROCESS of acquiring information about the frontier and the existence of established migration routes favored emigration from specific states and districts. They also created a tendency for people of similar backgrounds to settle near one another in new lands. Old family and neighborhood ties assured friendly receptions for the newcomers and assistance while establishing themselves on the frontier. A reflection of this continuity of social interaction may be found in the distribution of persons born in different states and living in Oregon. Immigrants settled among their own kind, often recreating culturally distinct neighborhoods similar to those from which they had come.

The earliest and by any measure the best defined and most famous of these "ethnic" districts was the French Canadian community of French Prairie (map 14). United by nationality, language, religion, and blood, this neighborhood was a model of clustering. Only a few households containing Canadians lay beyond its confines and these were situated almost always near sites formerly occupied by the Hudson's Bay Company.

Although the French Canadians produced the best example of a closed, culturally homogeneous community, they were not unique in their sense of neighborhood. Throughout much of the remaining foreign born and "ordinary" American population there also existed strong bonds between persons from similar localities, ties that often led them to join together and form recognizable districts. Even simple visual comparison of the household maps that follow indicates the location and character of these concentrations.

Because of their minor contribution to the frontier's population the foreign born, with the exception of the Canadians, were not differentiated by nationality, but were mapped as a single unit. The resulting sheet indicates that the group was largely urban in character (map 15). Although aliens amounted to only 3.8 percent of the total population, they accounted for 9.6 percent of the cities' inhabitants. Fully 60 percent of them lived in towns—25 percent in Oregon City alone. Rural households were few and scattered. Only north of Salem, between the Pudding and Willamette rivers was there any grouping, and there the settlers were mostly retired Hudson's Bay Company employees associated with the stronger French Canadian community. Elsewhere, three or four houses, clustered together along a prairie margin, comprised the largest number that could be found.

Settlers of New England extraction were in many respects similar to the foreign born. They too were chiefly men without families and were employed as laborers, clerks, merchants, and tradesmen. While accounting for only slightly more than 4 percent of all persons living in Oregon, they constituted in excess of 10 percent of the urban dwellers. In other words, New Englanders were almost two and a half times as common in towns as in the surrounding countryside.

Inasmuch as the men from the Northeast were a small minority and 58 percent of their number lived in urban areas, they were rarely found in the rural districts (map 16). Their single recognizable rural neighborhood was situated on the west Tualatin Plains, near the mouth of Gales Creek, and that cluster was largely due to the resettlement there of Protestant missionaries displaced from their stations east of the Cascades by the Cayuse Indian War. Otherwise, there were only inconsequential concentrations of several households on the Clackamas and Pudding rivers, between the Rickreall and Luckiamute, and in the logging camps near Astoria.

Emigrants from the Middle Atlantic states of New York, Pennsylvania, New Jersey, and Delaware labored at commercial pursuits in an urban setting. However, they also played an active role in the region's rural life. Generally they were widely scattered, but they did dominate several neighborhoods (map 17). In the Tualatin Valley, they associated with the New Englanders of the West Plains and nearby prairies. Below the Willa-

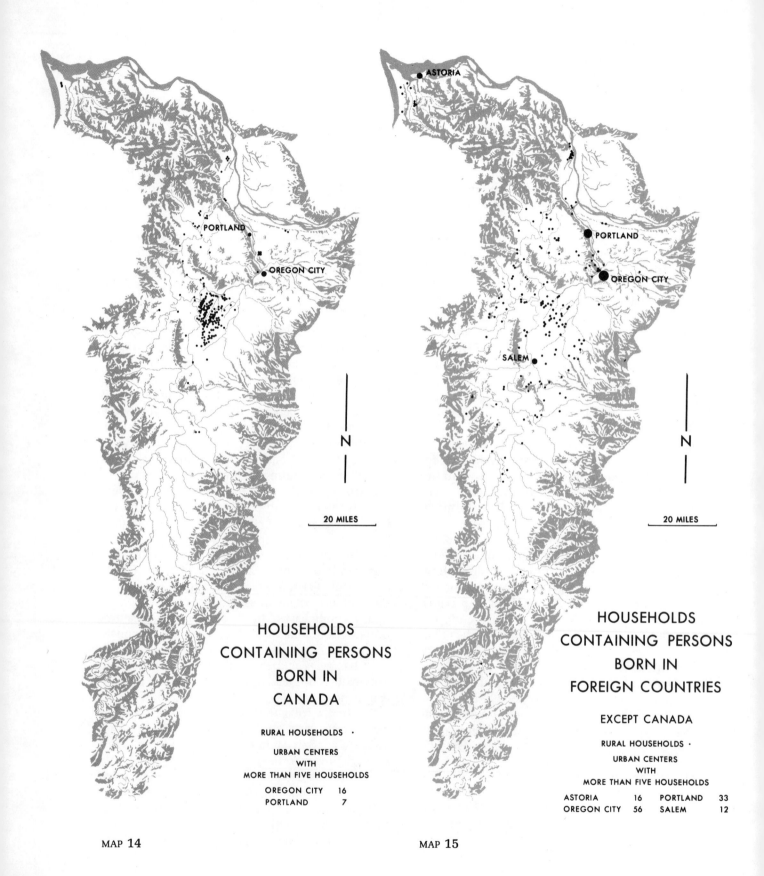

HOUSEHOLDS
CONTAINING PERSONS
BORN IN
CANADA

RURAL HOUSEHOLDS ·

URBAN CENTERS
WITH
MORE THAN FIVE HOUSEHOLDS

OREGON CITY   16
PORTLAND   7

MAP 14

HOUSEHOLDS
CONTAINING PERSONS
BORN IN
FOREIGN COUNTRIES

EXCEPT CANADA

RURAL HOUSEHOLDS ·

URBAN CENTERS
WITH
MORE THAN FIVE HOUSEHOLDS

ASTORIA   16   PORTLAND   33
OREGON CITY   56   SALEM   12

MAP 15

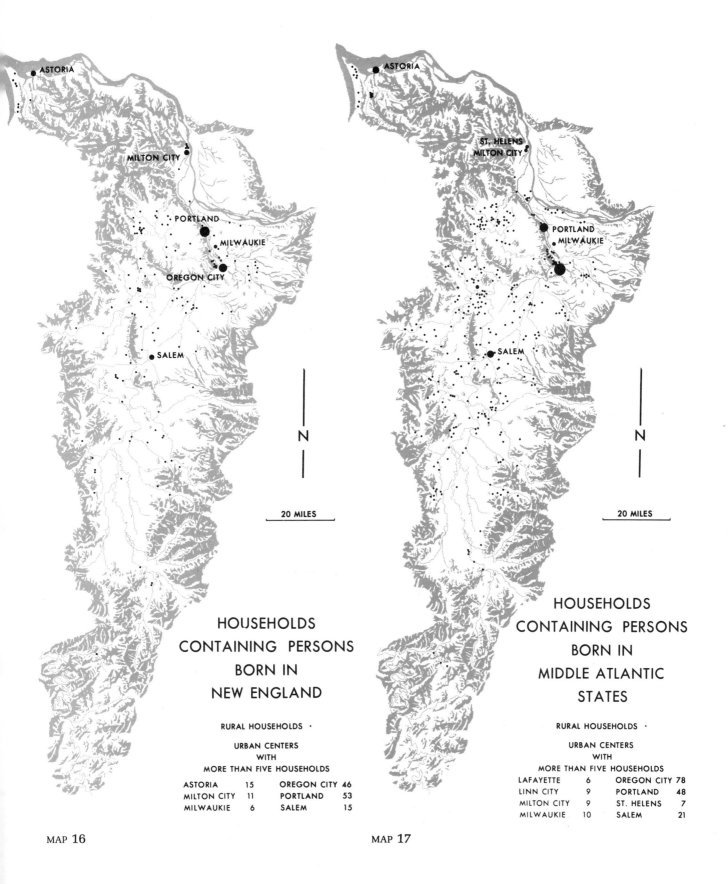

**HOUSEHOLDS
CONTAINING PERSONS
BORN IN
NEW ENGLAND**

RURAL HOUSEHOLDS ·

URBAN CENTERS
WITH
MORE THAN FIVE HOUSEHOLDS

ASTORIA	15	OREGON CITY	46
MILTON CITY	11	PORTLAND	53
MILWAUKIE	6	SALEM	15

MAP 16

**HOUSEHOLDS
CONTAINING PERSONS
BORN IN
MIDDLE ATLANTIC
STATES**

RURAL HOUSEHOLDS ·

URBAN CENTERS
WITH
MORE THAN FIVE HOUSEHOLDS

LAFAYETTE	6	OREGON CITY	78
LINN CITY	9	PORTLAND	48
MILTON CITY	9	ST. HELENS	7
MILWAUKIE	10	SALEM	21

MAP 17

mette Falls they lived on the south end of Sauvie Island, along the Clackamas River, and along the west bank of the Willamette River between Linn City and Portland. Above the falls, the largest group included twenty-five households between the Yamhill and Willamette rivers. Small clusters also lay along the Mollala, Pudding, Santiam, and Calapooya rivers. Another group, the Belknap settlement, nestled in the western foothills near the head waters of Muddy Creek.

Like the Middle Atlantic people, those from Ohio also inhabited both the urban and rural districts. In the towns they made up 9 percent of the population, whereas they contributed 7 percent of the entire Oregon population, again a slight imbalance in favor of the urban centers. Rural clusters were fairly common everywhere except Polk County (map 18). On the coast, and along the Willamette River immediately downstream from Linn City, Ohioans were connected with lumbering. Above the falls, concentrations existed on the East Tualatin Plains, upper Chehalem Valley, along the South Fork of the Yamhill and Mollala rivers, near Champoeg and along the west bank of the Pudding River, and southeast of Salem in the Waldo Hills. In the upper Willamette Valley, there were several fairly distinct family groups especially in Benton County. The largest of these was, again, the Belknap settlement. Equally well defined were clusters on the west bank of Muddy Creek, at the mouth of the Marys River, in Kings Valley, and north of Marysville. Smaller concentrations settled west of the South Santiam and in the headwaters of Oak Creek.

As can be seen in table 8, all other birth groups contributed proportionately less to the peopling of urban centers. Persons born along the Atlantic Seaboard south of Maryland most nearly approached the frontier average, since 23 percent of their number lived in towns. Not only were they more rural in their settlement habits, than the northerners, but also more widely scattered (map 19). People from Virginia, the Carolinas, Maryland, and Georgia lived in almost every district.

Kentuckians were likewise spread throughout the countryside (map 20). Their only large neighborhood was situated on the East Tualatin Plains. Elsewhere, they generally associated with settlers from the South Atlantic states. Small clusters of Kentuckians, usually related to one another, resided on Sauvie Island, the middle Tualatin River, upper Salt Creek, on either bank of the Santiam,

TABLE 8
Urban Population by State or Region of Origin

Birthplace	Number of Persons Living in Towns	Percent of Each State's Total Living in Towns
New England	286	58
Middle Atlantic	353	39
South Atlantic	177	23
Ohio	253	30
Indiana	135	19
Illinois	179	18
Kentucky	159	22
Missouri	339	15
Tennessee	46	12
Iowa	84	19
Foreign Born (excluding Canadians)	269	60
Total Urban Population	2,807	23.6[a]

[a]Percent of the total frontier population.
Source: Corrected United States Census, 1850.

across the Willamette River from Montieth's place (Albany), the headwaters of Oak Creek, along the lower course of the Mary's River, and far to the south between the forks of the Willamette. In addition, there were more general distributions in the Waldo Hills and along the Yamhill River.

Settlers born in Tennessee tended to be even more rural than their Kentucky brethren, only 12 percent of them living in towns. Although less numerous, they spread themselves widely, like other southerners (map 21). Their most distinct neighborhood was located in Polk County along Rickreall Creek. Other lesser communities existed just north of Salem, along the Luckiamute, on the California Road south of Marysville, in the Calapooya settlement, and, far to the south, on the Yoncalla.

The map of persons born in Indiana also shows a settlement pattern of wide dispersion punctuated by small aggregations of households (map 22). Hoosiers played no important role on the urban frontier; only 135, or 19 percent, resided in Oregon's small towns. In the rural districts, limited concentrations occurred in the Chehalem Valley, associated with pioneers from Virginia, North Carolina, and Kentucky; at the mouth of the Yamhill, in conjunction with those born in the Middle Atlantic states; southeast of Salem, near the junction of the Santiam and Willamette rivers; and in the Calapooya River Valley.

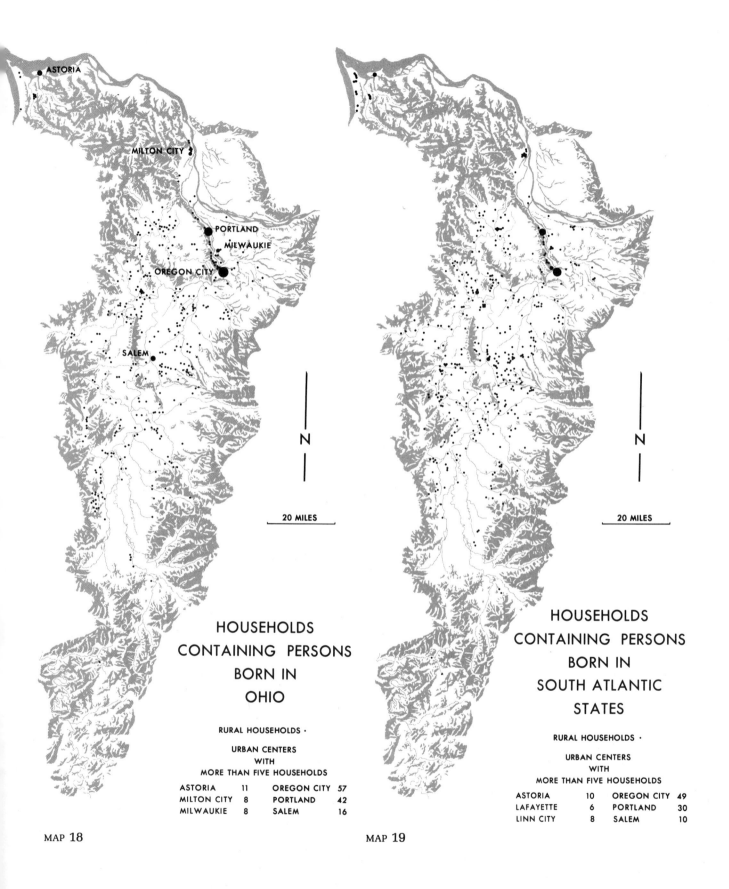

HOUSEHOLDS
CONTAINING PERSONS
BORN IN
OHIO

RURAL HOUSEHOLDS ·

URBAN CENTERS
WITH
MORE THAN FIVE HOUSEHOLDS

ASTORIA	11	OREGON CITY	57
MILTON CITY	8	PORTLAND	42
MILWAUKIE	8	SALEM	16

MAP 18

HOUSEHOLDS
CONTAINING PERSONS
BORN IN
SOUTH ATLANTIC
STATES

RURAL HOUSEHOLDS ·

URBAN CENTERS
WITH
MORE THAN FIVE HOUSEHOLDS

ASTORIA	10	OREGON CITY	49
LAFAYETTE	6	PORTLAND	30
LINN CITY	8	SALEM	10

MAP 19

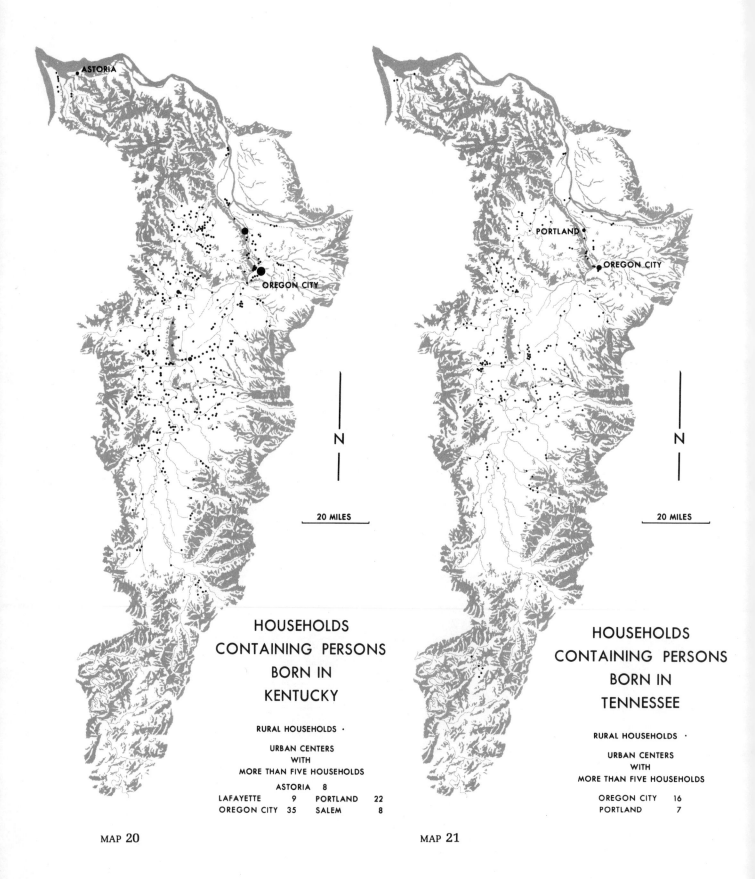

HOUSEHOLDS
CONTAINING PERSONS
BORN IN
KENTUCKY

RURAL HOUSEHOLDS ·

URBAN CENTERS
WITH
MORE THAN FIVE HOUSEHOLDS

ASTORIA   8
LAFAYETTE   9   PORTLAND   22
OREGON CITY   35   SALEM   8

MAP 20

HOUSEHOLDS
CONTAINING PERSONS
BORN IN
TENNESSEE

RURAL HOUSEHOLDS ·

URBAN CENTERS
WITH
MORE THAN FIVE HOUSEHOLDS

OREGON CITY   16
PORTLAND   7

MAP 21

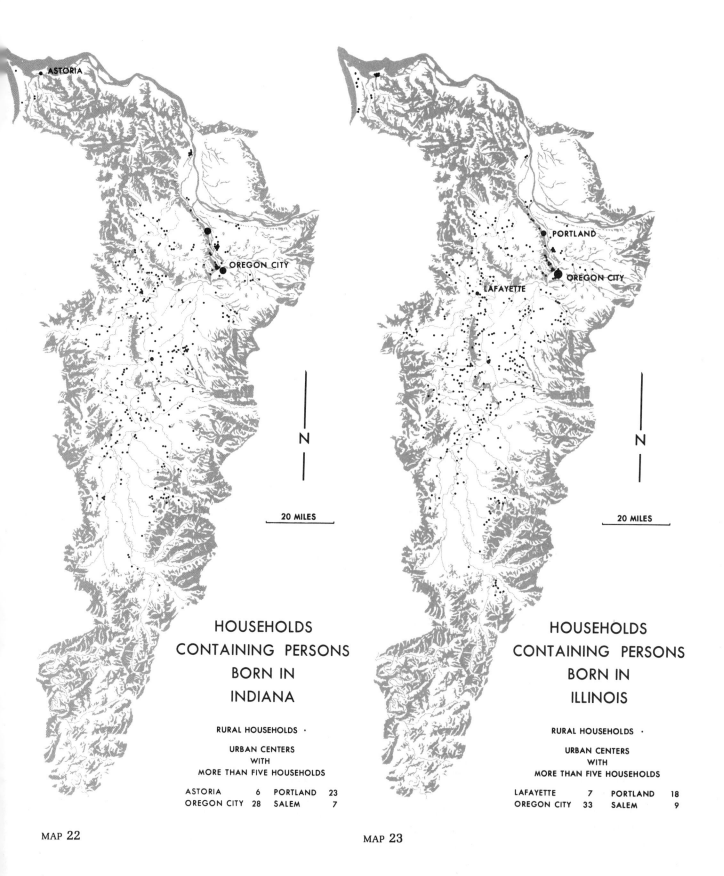

ASTORIA

OREGON CITY

HOUSEHOLDS
CONTAINING PERSONS
BORN IN
INDIANA

RURAL HOUSEHOLDS ·

URBAN CENTERS
WITH
MORE THAN FIVE HOUSEHOLDS

| ASTORIA | 6 | PORTLAND | 23 |
| OREGON CITY | 28 | SALEM | 7 |

MAP 22

PORTLAND

OREGON CITY

LAFAYETTE

HOUSEHOLDS
CONTAINING PERSONS
BORN IN
ILLINOIS

RURAL HOUSEHOLDS ·

URBAN CENTERS
WITH
MORE THAN FIVE HOUSEHOLDS

| LAFAYETTE | 7 | PORTLAND | 18 |
| OREGON CITY | 33 | SALEM | 9 |

MAP 23

N

20 MILES

N

20 MILES

Like the natives of Indiana, those of Illinois were basically rural people and were scattered throughout the country (map 23). They settled both in distinct groups and interspersed with other groups. Distinguishable neighborhoods were located along the Mollala River, in the upper Chehalem Valley, on the Yamhill River, in the Waldo Hills east of Salem, and at the mouth of Rickreall Creek. In the southern Willamette Valley, there were three concentrations: one at the mouth of the Santiam River related to persons born in Indiana, another on the south side of the Calapooya Valley and extending southward along the base of the hills, and a third between the forks of the Willamette River. This last was largely a single clan made up of adults from Kentucky and children born in Illinois.

The Iowans were less numerous and younger than other major Middle Western groups. Unlike the others, they were not so widely distributed (map 24). Many districts had only a few individuals born in Iowa, or none at all. Above the falls, only four aggregations existed. These included one of seven households on the upper Yamhill and Chehalem Valley divide, another less distinct concentration east of Salem, a third strung out along the prairie margins of northern Linn County, and a fourth confined to the Belknap settlement of central Benton County. This last group consisted almost entirely of children born to parents from the Middle Atlantic states.

The final and most numerous American group was the Missourians. Although in absolute terms they accounted for more urbanites than any other state, they had little propensity to settle in towns, approximately half the frontier average. Numerous Missouri farm families located on the lowlands of Sauvie Island and the Columbia River south of Fort Vancouver (map 25). Above the falls, they dominated the valleys of the Tualatin, Yamhill, Rickreall, Luckiamute, Calapooya, and Yoncalla rivers. They were also by far the largest group between the forks of the Santiam River and to the north through the Waldo Hills. In Polk County the concentration was exceedingly great. Along the Rickreall and Luckiamute more than 80 percent of the households included natives of Missouri. Only in a few districts like French Prairie did they form a minor element of the population.

Differential clustering of migrants, in both the old homelands and on the Oregon frontier, at least inferentially supports the view that overland migration and settlement were selective processes which did not randomly incorporate a true cross section of the American people. It also suggests that often the clan—not the individual—was the basic migratory unit. Absolute proof of these hypotheses, however, is difficult, for time has all but totally obscured the exact nature of the connections which existed between seemingly related households. Whether individuals were bound together by former acquaintance, economic interests, kinship, or mere chance cannot be determined by simple reference to historical materials. Because of their insubstantial and well-known nature personal relationships were seldom recorded and preserved. Then too, the mobility of the pioneer population and its aversion to being counted to some degree defied all attempts at comprehensive registration. The only surviving record of most persons on the frontier is the cryptic notation in the census schedule.

There are exceptions, of course, the most noteworthy being the fragmentary records of kinship found in old newspapers, obituaries, county and church archives, and other depositories of genealogical data. Many individuals who remained and prospered in the new land came to value their pioneer status highly and, through accident or design, exposed a small portion of their private lives to public scrutiny. Particularly attractive to the vanity of such persons were the biographical sections of the county and local histories, known as subscription histories, which for a modest sum ensured the subscriber's immortality. Buried in the bombast and the frozen portraits of these "mug books" are small bits of information—a wife's maiden name or the name of another relative—that when combined with other seemingly unrelated material yield at least a sketchy view of a community's blood ties.

During the course of this investigation, an alphabetical census list was produced for the systematic abstraction of genealogical data related to the Oregon pioneers. More than two hundred books and manuscripts were consulted and a large personal file developed. To simplify the problem of collecting information, emphasis was placed on the rural settlers of the Willamette Valley who had originated in the United States. These people made up the majority of the frontier population and were the most significant as migrants and as transformers of the landscape.

The genealogical survey was made to assess tentatively the importance of blood ties as a controlling force in the movement and settlement

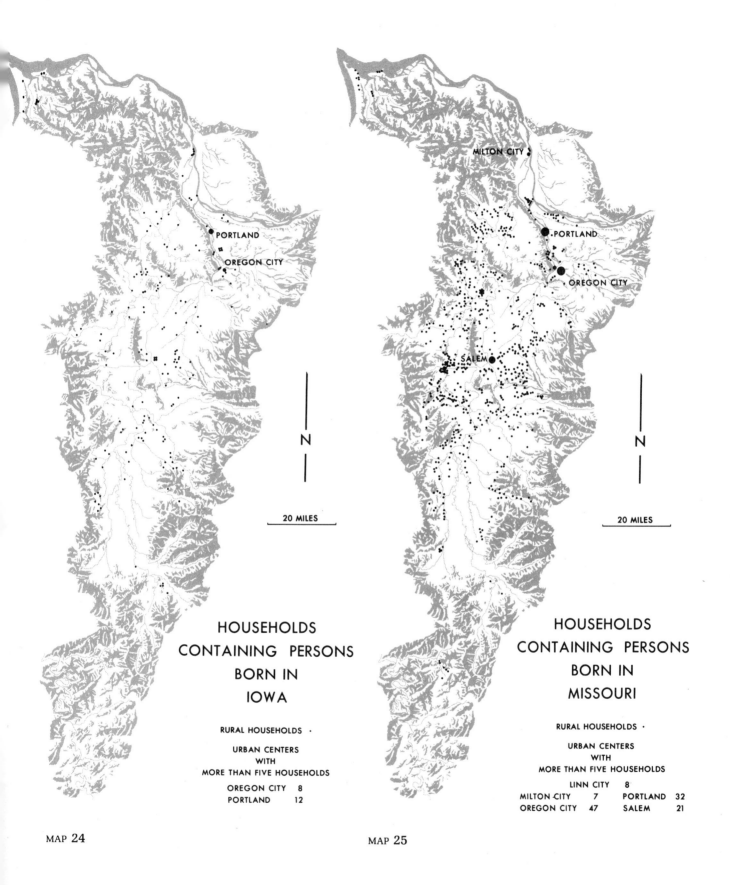

HOUSEHOLDS
CONTAINING PERSONS
BORN IN
IOWA

RURAL HOUSEHOLDS ·

URBAN CENTERS
WITH
MORE THAN FIVE HOUSEHOLDS
OREGON CITY   8
PORTLAND   12

MAP 24

HOUSEHOLDS
CONTAINING PERSONS
BORN IN
MISSOURI

RURAL HOUSEHOLDS ·

URBAN CENTERS
WITH
MORE THAN FIVE HOUSEHOLDS
LINN CITY   8
MILTON CITY   7   PORTLAND   32
OREGON CITY   47   SALEM   21

MAP 25

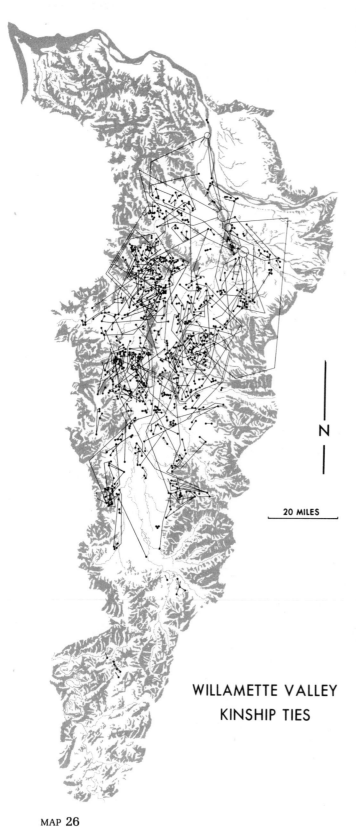

WILLAMETTE VALLEY
KINSHIP TIES

MAP 26

of people in the wilderness. If familial connections were numerous and close, then causative links might be proven to exist between (1) the way in which information about the frontier was acquired and decisions to migrate were made and (2) the role of the clan in determining the ethnic character and distribution of people on the frontier. It cannot be stressed too much that kinship, while perhaps the strongest tie between individuals, was merely one of several cohesive social bonds affecting the decisions of the Oregon pioneer. Church, fraternal, neighborhood, and business ties have been completely ignored. Neither can the extreme sketchiness of the existing records be overemphasized. Any conclusions based upon written materials must, *ipso facto*, greatly underestimate the true complexity of the connections in a primitive and partially illiterate society.

Rather than attempting a tiresome discussion of specific pioneer genealogies, this study sets forth a graphic portrayal of kinship links between households, as this seems to be the most comprehensible means of approaching the material. The resulting map is both simple and confusing: simple in that it shows only the most direct blood connection where there are several possible, confusing in that even with very inadequate data hundreds of interlocking ties must be mapped (map 26). The final effect suggests a plate of spaghetti through which the course of a single strand can be followed with the greatest difficulty.

The unevenness in the frequency and distribution of connections in several of the valley's districts is due in large measure to inadequate documentation in the northern and eastern counties. If complete genealogical data were available, the number of ties would probably increase at least two- or threefold, and their distribution would be more even throughout the frontier. Nevertheless, even grossly inadequate materials indicate that at least 45 percent of the Willamette Valley's 1,500 rural households had blood ties with one or more other residences in 1850.

Although the numerous tangled lines of the master map impress us with the ubiquity and complexity of the connections, they do not clearly show the clustering so important in the establishment of definable ethnic neighborhoods. To obtain some order from the confusion, all but the lines leading directly or indirectly from a single household were eliminated. The residence chosen belonged to Lewis Rodgers, household 143 in the manuscript census schedules for Yamhill County.

Rodgers was an illiterate native of Indiana who emigrated from Iowa in 1846, a year after two of his sons, Clark and William, left for Oregon. In October of 1846, he settled a claim in the Chehalem Valley. Five of his adult children also established themselves in Yamhill County. By 1850, Rodgers was connected through marriage to the neighboring Jacob Shuck and Stephen Nelson families. They were related in turn to other households near and distant.

The trace includes over seventy households and several hundred persons. As map 27 indicates, they were not widely dispersed, but were concentrated in four more or less distinct groups. In the three northern clusters, all ties were through kinship and all shared a basically southern heritage. In the fourth case, the Belknap settlement of Benton County, the connection was merely through a shared residence, not marriage. In contrast to the other three, this southernmost group consisted almost wholly of northern stock, who came to Oregon by way of New York, Ohio, and Iowa.

Multiplied over and over again, the neighborhood was one of the most basic associations of rural frontier life, a union of persons with similar backgrounds in small, fairly homogeneous communities, each slightly different from the rest. The frontier experience in Oregon was not one that broke down existing social structures. If anything, it tended to strengthen them. Through membership in a clan all the necessities of human survival in the wilderness were most certainly obtained.

The ramifications of this meeting of individual needs with group resources were great. First, it excluded many outsiders from the overland migrations. Secondly, it introduced a new and unseen factor into the decision-making process which tended to restrict the pioneer's ultimate choice of location. The precise situation of a person often depended as much upon the location of previously established social contacts as it did upon other more apparent physical and economic factors.

Those who found family and friends at their destination were easily assimilated into rural society. Those who did not, or worse, were somehow different, were not taken in so quickly. The single man, the Yankee, or the foreign born might function as a laborer in the rural districts, but without ready access to community sympathy and thus to shelter, credit, and cooperative labor it was difficult for him to become a farmer. The most

direct route of entry was for the outsider to marry into a country family, but many were unwilling or unable to follow this course. For most of these individuals, survival depended upon their successful participation in a money economy where simple financial considerations substituted for those of family and friends. Thus, the stage was set for the development of two dissimilar frontiers—one, a rural frontier characterized by clans of westerners; the other, an urban frontier drawing its members disproportionately from the ranks of unmarried men from the Northeast or abroad.

Students of the American Far West concerned with the investigation of purely temporal matters have seldom recognized this basic division of Oregon's frontier population into two groups, a division fundamental enough to affect the social and political histories of the towns and countryside. Failing to see the geographic nature of the division in the Northwest and perhaps elsewhere, many researchers have erroneously combined the two groups and analyzed them as a single unit. The result has been an amazingly wide spectrum of opinion concerning even so basic a matter as the true demographic character of the pioneers.

When the age-sex characteristics of the entire enumerated population are plotted at one year intervals, the resulting pyramid describes a normal shape in which the young outnumber their elders (figure 1). In the two youngest age groups there is some reduction in numbers, indicating a decline in the birth rate, but this aberration may be accounted for by the departure of husbands to the California mines during 1848 and 1849 and by the fact that all Clackamas County infants were counted as being at least one year old.

Perhaps the most impressive aspect of the pyramid is the imbalance of the sexes. Of a total population of 11,873 persons, 7,202 were men and only 4,671 were women—a sex ratio of 154.2 males per 100 females. As the skewed diagram demonstrates, the preponderance of men was not evenly distributed with respect to age, but was concentrated among adults above twenty years. In this group the ratios of men to women ranged between approximately 202 and 264 per 100.

Considering the relatively greater social mobility of men in nineteenth-century America, the ratio of men to women on the Oregon frontier is not particularly remarkable. If anything, it is perhaps less than might have been expected. Noteworthy is the great difference between the sex composition of rural and urban areas. By reclassifying the age

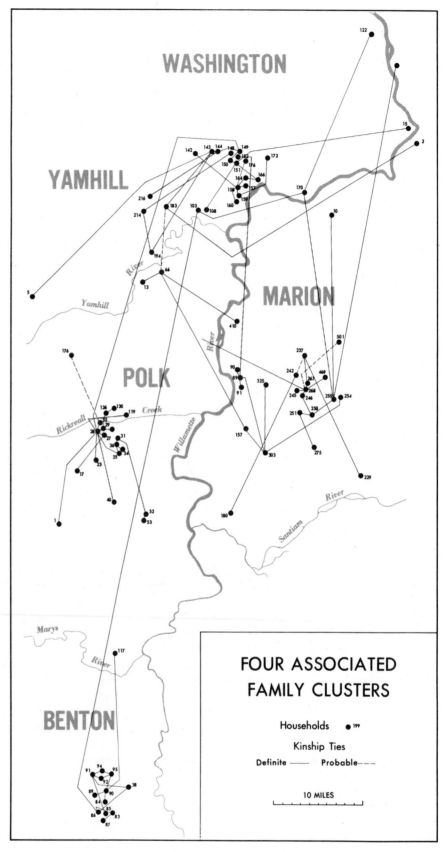

WASHINGTON

YAMHILL

MARION

POLK

BENTON

FOUR ASSOCIATED
FAMILY CLUSTERS

Households   ●¹⁹⁹

Kinship Ties

Definite ———   Probable ----

10 MILES

MAP 27

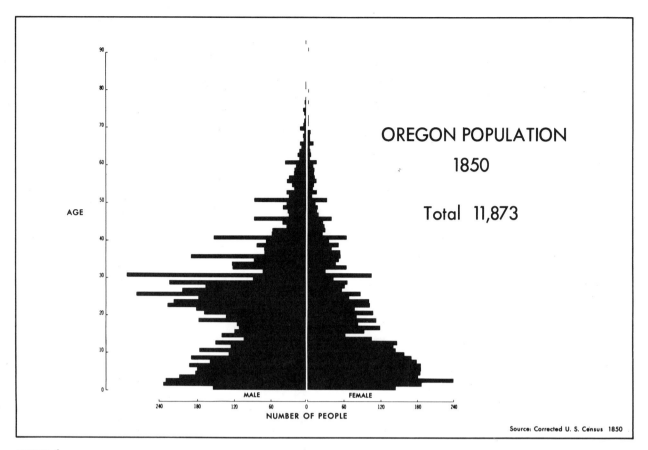

FIGURE 1

groups at five-year intervals and enlarging the horizontal scale, the author has made a series of exaggerated pyramids emphasizing this difference (figure 2). It is immediately apparent that although the distribution was skewed in favor of men in both town and country, the imbalance was significantly greater in the former. Of the 2,789 identified urbanites residing south of the Columbia, 1,937 or 69.4 percent were males. In contrast, 5,265 of the 9,084 rural inhabitants were men—a more equitable 57.9 percent.

Inasmuch as the urban population was concentrated in several centers in the north, not evenly distributed throughout the region, the ratio of men to women differed widely from one district to another. This becomes very clear when separate pyramids are constructed for each of the eight counties (map 28). In urban Clatsop, Washington, and Clackamas counties, sex ratios were respectively 274.8, 210.4, and 154.6 men per 100 women, whereas in the entirely rural settings of Benton and Linn counties, they were 126.8 and 126.4 per 100.

Just as the character of county populations varied with the degree of urbanization, the towns themselves also revealed very real demographic contrasts. By defining the limits of the several centers and then constructing pyramids for each, the varying importance of age and sex may be graphically compared (map 29). In the towns that had sprung up along navigable waterways with the development of an important lumber and grain trade serving the California mines, single men were overwhelmingly dominant. At Astoria, Milton City, and Portland they outnumbered women more than three to one. Farther inland the small rural trading towns of Salem and Lafayette were more balanced.

As with the general population, the sex characteristics of the towns' populations reflected the varying predominance of adult males, especially between the ages of twenty and twenty-nine. In this group men outnumbered women 7.6 to one at Astoria, 9.5 to one at St. Helens, 6.8 to one at Milton City, and 9.2 to one at Portland. In contrast, the ratio at Salem was 3.1 to one, and

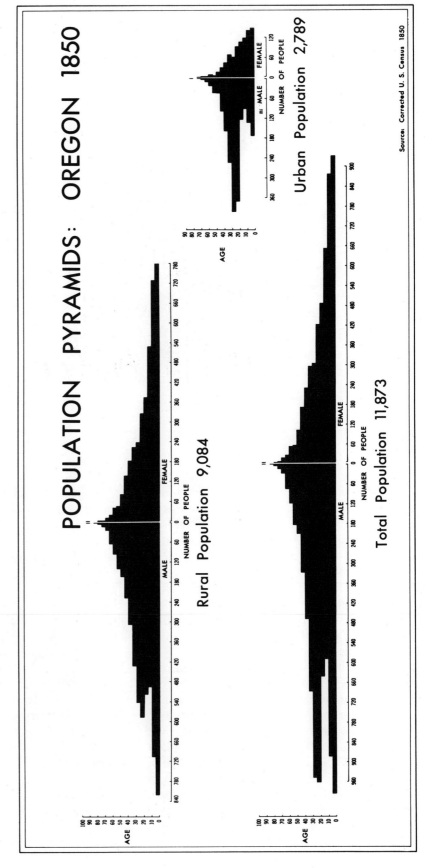

POPULATION PYRAMIDS: OREGON 1850

Rural Population 9,084

Urban Population 2,789

Total Population 11,873

Source: Corrected U. S. Census 1850

FIGURE 2

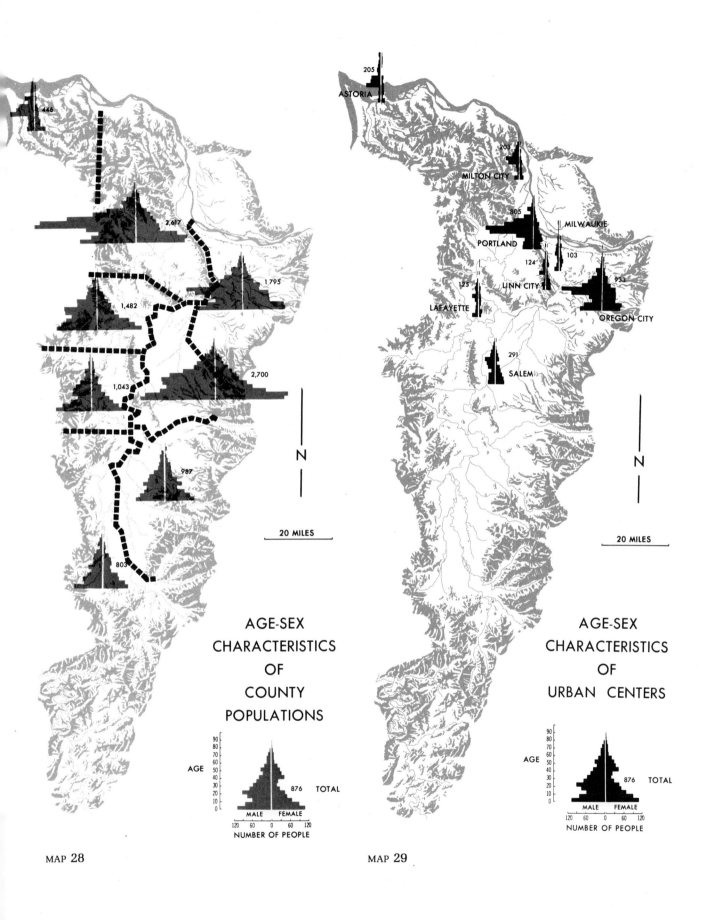

AGE-SEX
CHARACTERISTICS
OF
COUNTY
POPULATIONS

AGE-SEX
CHARACTERISTICS
OF
URBAN CENTERS

20 MILES

20 MILES

AGE

876 TOTAL

MALE FEMALE
120 60 0 60 120
NUMBER OF PEOPLE

AGE

876 TOTAL

MALE FEMALE
120 60 0 60 120
NUMBER OF PEOPLE

MAP 28

MAP 29

ASTORIA 205

MILTON CITY 203

PORTLAND 805

MILWAUKIE

124

103

LINN CITY

LAFAYETTE 125

OREGON CITY 933

SALEM 291

446

2,617

1,795

1,482

1,043

2,700

987

803

that at Lafayette was 2.6 to one.

The propensity for young, single men to reside more in some communities than in others is attributable to the varying economic attractions of each. In towns along the Columbia River the stimuli of trade and milling were augmented by competition between town speculators. Promoters at St. Helens, Milton City, Portland, and Milwaukie hired men to improve their townsites. Forests had to be cleared from the land and lumber sawed. Warehouses, stores, and residences were raised and many other improvements made. To divert trade from their competitors, boomers even subsidized road construction.

The immediate result of all this activity was the creation of new jobs. In the May 30, 1850 issue of the *Oregon Spectator*, the Milton City group advised, "50 LABORERS WANTED to Complete the road from Milton to the Tualatin Plains." On December 5, 1850, Milton City's owners again advertised in the *Oregon Spectator*, "We can give permanent employment to quite a number of hands during the winter." By concentrating capital and investing it in such physical improvements the New England merchants attracted men of similar backgrounds—men whose survival depended wholly upon the money economy of commerce and industry.

In the north where milling and other economic pursuits were commonly carried on outside the towns, single adult males were of some local importance even in the country. Up valley in the more distant agricultural districts to the south, however, the influence of money gave way to that of barter and the clan. Unattached men became less numerous, and the frontier population was increasingly dominated by large families.

CHAPTER 5

Physical Environment and Settlement

ALTHOUGH social connections and the process of acquiring information about the frontier affected the Oregon pioneers' choice of residence, in particular influencing the location of households relative to one another, other factors influenced the specific siting of frontier farmsteads with respect to the physical environment. To begin to understand why men established their farms in certain places in preference to others, attention must be given to some of the characteristics of the wilderness which they confronted.

One of the more popular topics of frontier scholarship has been the interaction of the pioneer and the native inhabitants. Notwithstanding the attention paid to them by local historians, the Indians of the Willamette Valley and lower Columbia were of little direct consequence to American settlement during the 1840s. Altogether they probably numbered fewer than five hundred at the time of the first federal census. East of the Cascades and south of the Umpqua River the Indians were numerous and determined adversaries, but in the area of settlement they posed no threat.

The situation could scarcely have been otherwise. For more than a century the tribes of western Oregon had been exposed to and greatly reduced by the corrosive effects of imported disease. Even before Lewis and Clark's arrival on the coast smallpox had taken thousands of lives, and venereal disease introduced by coastal traders had infected the Chinook villages along the Columbia River.

Besides smallpox and venereal disease, the Indians suffered from malaria, influenza, diphtheria, and a host of other illnesses. George B. Roberts, a clerk for the Hudson's Bay Company at Fort Vancouver, wrote of many cases of leprosy. He also remembered that with the American immigrations, "every fall the Indians were excited as to what new ill was to come—whooping cough, measles, typhoid fever, etc. . . . . All these things we think so lightly of now, scourged the poor

Indians dreadfully."[1] In the fall of 1850 cholera was introduced, but by that time very few natives remained to be infected.

Although the Indians had relatively little direct effect upon the location of rural settlement in western Oregon, their influence through the modification of the natural vegetation was great. When white men first came to Oregon, immense forests covered most of the country on either side of the Columbia River. Surveys made by the United States Surveyor General in the early 1850s show that above the falls of the Willamette, timber extended with few interruptions southward beyond the Mollala River. South of the great eastern bend of the Willamette River on the level land west of the Pudding River, the countryside opened up as narrow fingers of grass broke the monotony of the trees (map 30). Where the prairies were more numerous and extensive towards the south, government surveyors indicated that the character of the intervening woodland also changed. The dense coniferous forest was confined increasingly to the higher mountain slopes or the wet terrain immediately adjacent to the streams; and in its place appeared oak woodland and savanna-like "oak openings." In both associations, the Oregon oak (*Quercus garryana*) was the dominant species, and in both there was usually an absence of shrubby growth.

South of the Santiam River an open plain spread in all directions to the limits of the valley. The vast expanse of grass was broken only by an occasional shallow swale along the margins of which grew scattered ash trees and oaks. Wooded strips containing vine maple, ash, oak, maple, and occasional Douglas fir followed the banks of the Santiam, Calapooya, and Willamette rivers out into the valley, while the floodplains of these streams' upper courses were often characterized by small segmented prairies.

West of the Willamette River, the valley floor was more restricted, and as a consequence the seasonally-inundated plain between the main

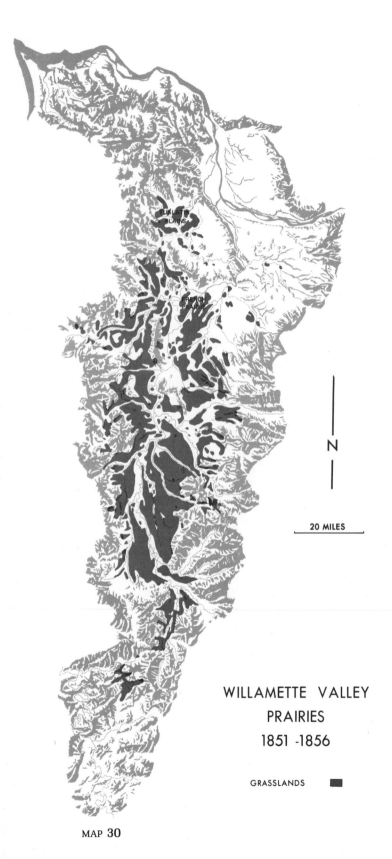

WILLAMETTE VALLEY
PRAIRIES
1851 -1856

GRASSLANDS ■

MAP 30

stream and the Long Tom River was the only extensive grassland. Northward, smaller, more broken prairies clothed the valley floors of the Marys, Luckiamute, Yamhill, and Tualatin rivers. Oak woodland was much more common on the low hills which separated the drainage basins of the major west side tributaries.

From the time of John Jacob Astor's hunters, the prairies of the Willamette Valley excited the imaginations of travelers. Well-endowed with wild game, they soon became favorite hunting grounds. During the lean years of the Pacific and North West fur companies, armed parties frequently hunted the area for deer and elk. The open grasslands provided the most rapid avenues of travel, and on one of these plains, French Prairie, the first substantial settlement of retired Hudson's Bay Company employees was begun.

From their earliest days of exploration most travelers ascribed the prairies' existence to Indian burning. During the dry season each year, the natives purposely set large fires in the grass and woodlands. Often they burned over hundreds of square miles. During his journey southward through the valley with a party of trappers in the fall of 1826, David Douglas, the noted botanist, wrote of the lands west of the Willamette River: "Most parts of the country burned; only on little patches in the valleys and on the flats near the low hills that verdure is to be seen. Some of the natives tell me it is done for the purpose of urging the deer to frequent certain parts, to feed, which they leave unburned, and of course, they are easily killed. Others say that it is done in order they might the better find wild honey and grasshoppers, which both serve as articles of winter food."[2]

Despite the reduction of Indian population, fires continued to spread annually across the countryside throughout the 1830s and 1840s. On the great grassland south of the Santiam River in June 1841, Jason Lee reported that his party "moved gently over the plains; but the fire had stripped them of the verdure, and we could not find grass enough for our horses." Two days later in the hills south of the valley he noted, "The fire, which usually allows no part of the country to escape its ravages, for more than two or three years at a time, was making terrible destruction among the underbrush. The smoke in some places was almost suffocating. . . ."[3]

Early American settlers also witnessed the holocausts. In 1844 several Applegate families crossed the Willamette River into what is now Polk County and established a camp on Salt Creek: "While camped at this place, as autumn approached and the grass became very dry, high and thick, the Indians set out fires, and the whole country was burned over. The fire at this time was started in the lower part of Yamhill County, came up the valley with great speed, being fanned by the northwest wind, leeping Salt Creek and on to our encampment, which was with great difficulty saved."[4]

Rapid settlement of the grasslands and an even more rapid decline of the native population in the 1840s reduced the number of conflagrations. Journals document that Indian burning was all but a thing of the past in most areas by 1850 and reforestation had begun. During the 1840s, however, few seedlings had yet appeared on the prairie margins, and the prehistoric grasslands and oak savanna were still intact. More than any other aspect of the physical landscape, the distribution of these two plant communities, especially the treeless prairies, determined the location of rural settlement throughout the Willamette Valley. Just as the French Canadians made their farms in the first sizable grassland upstream from the falls of the Willamette, so the American hunters and those who followed sought the prairies and settled upon them.

By 1850 the correlation between vegetation and settlement was firmly established (map 31). More than 90 percent of the farms had been established within the grasslands. Detailed studies made using the original cadastral surveys of the United States Surveyor General show that the location of the rural population in every district was largely determined by the distribution of vegetation. At French Prairie, nearly all the Canadian farms were located within the grassland, as were those of the Americans who settled on the Tualatin Plains and Howell's Prairie. Claims established later in the upper portions of the Willamette Valley repeated the pattern. Whether along the banks of a major stream, such as the Santiam, or in the more restricted bottoms of a small west side tributary, the pioneers located in grasslands.

Many of the fewer than ten percent who chose to settle outside the prairies laid out claims in the oak openings and other sparsely timbered areas which, although classified in the early surveys as woodland, were quite open and easily cleared for cultivation. The remainder of the forest claims were associated with either logging operations, or with water-driven mills, located along the

MAP 31

OREGON
POPULATION
1850

URBAN POPULATION CENTERS

Astoria............205	Milwaukie.......103
Lafayette.........125	Oregon City...933
Linn City.........124	Portland...........805
Milton City......141	Salem................291
St. Helens.......62	

SIZE OF RURAL HOUSEHOLDS

· 1-3 persons   • 9-15
· 4-8   • more than 15

Willamette River and its tributaries. Prior to 1850, probably less than a dozen farms in all of western Oregon south of the Columbia were hewn out of anything approaching dense forest. Thousands of acres of unclaimed prairie made forest clearing unnecessary, and except for land near the few small lumber mills, timber had little monetary value. In addition, the floor of much of the denser forest in the north was overrun by ferns which proved almost impossible to eradicate.

Although the pioneer farmers avoided cultivating the wooded lands and situated their cultivated fields in the prairies, they also depended upon the resources of the forest. Their most pressing need was wood. Except for farming, woodworking was the most common occupation in Oregon. The first substantial home was almost invariably made from logs, sometimes hewn, but more commonly not. The other structures of the frontier were also made with an axe or saw. Carts, furniture, fences, tools, agricultural machinery, and even dishes were fabricated from wood. And, when all these were completed, there remained an endless need for firewood.

The woodlands were also used by the settlers who turned their swine loose to feed on acorns and camas roots. From the forest the women and children gathered abundant harvests of wild berries and hazel nuts. Hazel and willow switches were cut and twisted to make pliable withes that substituted for wire or twine. Even the leaves of some shrubs were brewed for tea.

Dependence upon the natural resources of both the forest and the cultivated fields led settlers to seek locations along the margins of these two different environments. Everywhere on the frontier the first lands claimed were those on the prairie margins adjacent to the forest. More often than not the farmsteads themselves were situated within a few hundred feet of the trees. Travelers passing through the central portions of the larger prairies encountered few habitations. They might come upon a fence, some livestock, a cultivated field, and perhaps even a lone dwelling, but in most districts only the smokey gray plumes rising from cabins hidden in the shadows of the forest's edge and the fields along the prairies' margins indicated the settled condition of the country.

Recognizing the immigrants' marked bias for claims that included both prairie and woodland, it is not surprising that throughout the 1840s they generally avoided those areas dominated by one or the other. In the forests north of the French settlement there was almost no rural population. Most of those who resided in the northern districts were townspeople living in settlements developed subsequent to the discovery of gold in California. Speculative optimism created by the new demands for Oregon wheat and timber, had given birth to Portland, Milwaukie, Milton City, and St. Helens, and numerous mills had been established below the falls of the Willamette (map 32).

Just as rural settlers bypassed the wooded north, they also avoided the great treeless plains south of the Santiam River. Farms were established only around the periphery of the grassland, and even there the pioneers seem to have preferred the upland margins to the richer land adjacent to the Willamette River. Initially this choice is somewhat difficult to understand. Without question the immigrants appreciated the superior quality of alluvial soil. This is indicated by their locations on the better ground along the South Fork of the Santiam River, Oak Creek, and the Calapooya River. Yet, the records of the Surveyor General indicate that by 1849 only nine claims had been settled along the wooded margins of the Willamette River and its tributary the Muddy River. By that same date more than five times as many claims were to be found to the east, strung out along the base of the foothills.

The early settlers' avoidance of lands adjacent to the Willamette River can be partially ascribed to fear of high water. In 1844 James Clyman recorded in his diary that "considerable injury was done by the late Freshet heard of 1000 or Twelv Hundred bushel of wheat being lost in the graneries on the low grounds of the Wilhamet Likewise large lots of fencing and in some instances hogs and other stock being drowned or carried away by the water."[5] Driftwood and watermarks on trees testified that every several years the river flooded its bottoms and lower terraces, and for men long accustomed to the vagaries of midwestern streams such signs were usually sufficient deterrents to settlement. Some had already suffered serious economic loss in the Missouri and Mississippi river floods and had no wish to repeat the experience. Nathan King was an immigrant of 1845 whose entire farm had been destroyed by the great Missouri River flood of 1844. High water drove this man and his family west, and after spending the first winter on the Tualatin Plains he sought a claim which could never be similarly threatened. His choice was a small valley on the upper Luckiamute River, more than fifteen miles west of the Willamette River.

Another equally repellent feature of the lower sections of the valley was the swampy, mosquito-infested bottoms upstream from Champoeg. These were rightly perceived to be potential sources of malaria. To avoid the disease, many families from the bottomlands of the Missouri, Illinois, and Des Moines rivers took up claims several miles from the river. This combined with a general preference for spring water (which was most commonly available near the foothills) and friable, easily plowed soils predisposed farmers to settle along the higher margins of the valley where grass and forest met.

Rapid settlement of these prairie borders began with the arrival of the first great migration in the fall of 1843. After wintering in and around Oregon City, the Americans fanned out to make new homes. The smaller grasslands south of the French settlement and along the Tualatin River attracted the larger number of newcomers. Daniel Waldo initiated settlement of the open hill land east of the Willamette River, and John Howell established the first claim in the openings behind the Methodist Mission. Cabins were erected along Mill Creek and north of the Santiam River, and a new southern limit of white habitation on the west side was established by the Applegates on Salt Creek. In addition significant settlement began along the edges of the extensive prairies above the falls of the Yamhill River.

In each succeeding year the pattern of 1843–44 was repeated. A few of the early arrivals established claims in the fall, while the greater number of each migration remained in Oregon City or put up with some farmer or family friend. In the spring, those who were able journeyed up valley searching for a suitable claim site. Each year farms were begun further southward. In 1845 the valley of Rickreall Creek was first settled, and in 1846 families entered the valleys of the Luckiamute and Marys rivers. In that later year permanent settlements were also first made south of the Santiam River in what is today Linn County.

The opening of a new immigrant road from Fort Hall through Nevada and Southern Oregon to the upper end of the Willamette Valley in 1846 stimulated settlement in the south. In 1847, Eugene Skinner brought his family to the present site of Eugene and established a farm. The follow-

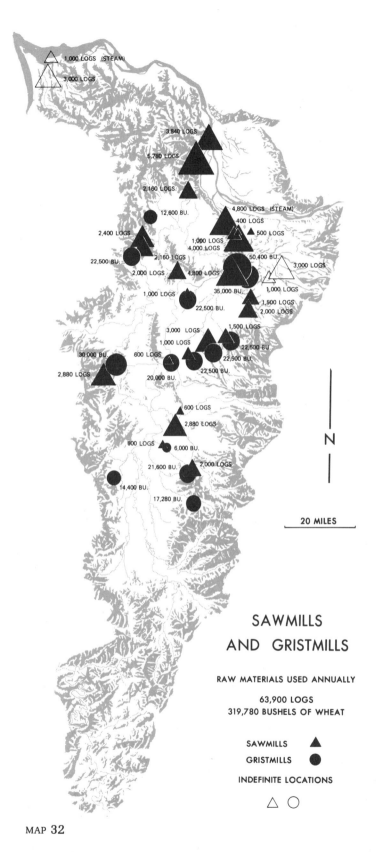

1,000 LOGS (STEAM)
3,000 LOGS
3,840 LOGS
6,780 LOGS
2,160 LOGS
12,600 BU.
4,800 LOGS (STEAM)
400 LOGS
500 LOGS
2,400 LOGS
1,000 LOGS
4,000 LOGS
50,400 BU.
22,500 BU.
2,160 LOGS
2,000 LOGS
4,800 LOGS
3,000 LOGS
1,000 LOGS
35,000 BU.
1,500 LOGS
2,000 LOGS
22,500 BU.
3,000 LOGS
1,500 LOGS
1,000 LOGS
600 LOGS
22,500 BU.
30,000 BU.
22,500 BU.
2,880 LOGS
20,000 BU.
22,500 BU.
600 LOGS
2,880 LOGS
800 LOGS
6,000 LOGS
21,600 BU.
2,000 LOGS
14,400 BU.
17,280 BU.

N

20 MILES

SAWMILLS
AND GRISTMILLS

RAW MATERIALS USED ANNUALLY

63,900 LOGS
319,780 BUSHELS OF WHEAT

SAWMILLS ▲
GRISTMILLS ●

INDEFINITE LOCATIONS

△ ○

MAP 32

ing year groups of families settled back from the upper Long Tom River, on prairies between the Coast and Middle forks of the Willamette, and far to the south on the Yoncalla River. In less than five years the American frontiersmen had pushed the limits of civilization beyond the confines of the Willamette Valley and the Columbia River borderlands.

CHAPTER 6

Frontier Economy and Land

THROUGHOUT the 1840s, the single most common characteristic of the immigrants was their poverty. Many underestimated the length of the overland journey and the obstacles they had to overcome. With few boats on the lower Columbia, hundreds of families lost everything at the Cascades, while others threatened with entrapment in the mountains by winter snows were forced to abandon their possessions. Men who had expected to establish farms during the first fall found themselves without any means of supporting their families. Livestock, wagons, and implements were lost, and in this time of need even the seed for the first year's crop was often eaten.

Down from the mountains came the straggling parties of the first great migrations. Starving and suffering from the cold and seemingly endless rain, they entered the fabled valley of the Willamette. Promises of free land, bountiful crops, and improved health were forgotten as fathers listened in desperation to their children crying for food. Unlike most of the earlier settlers, those of 1842 and 1843 had no formal connections with either the Hudson's Bay Company or the Methodist Missions. As a result, there was insufficient opportunity to plan for their needs. Neither institution had any reason to welcome the newcomers. For the company such a large colony of foreign nationals could only mean an end to the fur trade and British domination of the Columbia River. Similarly, the Methodists feared the new arrivals, for although they were Americans, they were not respectable New Englanders who could be counted on to support the economic and political interests of the Mission.

The displeasure of the missionaries with the westerners was first displayed at The Dalles mission, where they apparently refused to sell food to the immigrants or to help them in any way. Daniel Waldo later remembered, "Jason Lee played the devil up at the Dalles. He said the Mission had always ruled the country, and if there were any persons in the immigration who did not like to be ruled by the Mission they might find a country elsewhere to go to. It got all over the country, of course, very quickly. That made war with the missionaries at once."[1]

The Methodists' refusal to offer anything but begrudging and limited assistance placed the immigrants in a precarious situation, for only the Hudson's Bay Company, the very agency of British power in Oregon against which most Americans held the greatest prejudice, possessed resources sufficient to alleviate their immediate suffering and assist them in establishing farms. Fortunately for all concerned, Chief Factor McLoughlin extended credit to the destitute and opened the company's storehouses to the Americans' needs for the next two years. In defense of his action the chief factor later wrote:

When the immigration of 1842 came, we had enough breadstuffs in the country for one year, but as the immigrants reported that next season there would be a greater immigration, it was evident if there was not a proportionate increase of seed sown in 1843 and 1844, there would be a famine in the country in 1845, which would lead to trouble, as those that had families, to save them from starvation, would be obliged to have recourse to violence to get food for them. To avert this I freely supplied the immigrants of 1843 and 1844 with the necessary articles to open farms and by these means avoided the evils. In short I afforded every assistence to the immigrants so long as they required it, and by management I kept peace in the country.[2]

To those in need and able to work, McLoughlin offered jobs at Fort Vancouver and at his Oregon City claim, improving both the company's holdings and his own personal property. The small village established at the falls of the Willamette River by similarly employed men of the 1842 migration grew in size and importance as the latest arrivals erected cabins and other temporary shelters. Throughout the winter they worked at the mill or in the timber along the Clackamas and lower Willamette rivers. Dozens of men supported their families in this fashion during those first several months and, by making shingles, earned capital to start farms.

As the size of the American colony increased

the settlers' need for company assistance rapidly diminished. Seed loaned to the immigrants of 1842, 1843, and 1844 returned harvests sufficient to feed both the established population and needy newcomers. Each winter the populace was divided into these two dissimilar economic groups. On one hand were prospering farmers who after several seasons' effort were finally producing crops in excess of their families' needs, and on the other were those impoverished by their recent journey. Remembering this division, Peter Burnett, an immigrant of 1843 and early settler on the Tualatin Plains wrote:

At any public gathering, it was easy to distinguish the new from the old settlers. They were lank, lean, hungry, and tough. We were ruddy, ragged, and rough. They were dressed in broadcloth, wore linen-bosomed shirts and black cravats; while we wore very coarse patched clothes; for the art of patching was understood to perfection in Oregon. But while they dressed better than we did, we fed better than they. Of the two we were rather the more independent. They wanted our provisions, while we wanted their materials for clothing.[3]

Circumstances were such that the old pioneers were forced to take in the new, for like McLoughlin before them they realized that good public order depended upon their charity. Property was held almost in common, and the pioneer who refused to assist his less fortunate fellows was soon isolated from the community. Ameliorating what was at best a trying situation was the fact that a large number of each season's new arrivals were friends or relatives who had been attracted to Oregon by the letters of those who had preceded them.

Peter Burnett could hardly complain about his brother William's family, which came in the fall of 1846 and lived with him for nine months. Giving up stores to itinerant strangers, however, was another matter, about which he sometimes grumbled.

Many of the men emigrants were childish, most of them discouraged, and all of them more or less embarrassed. There was necessarily, under the circumstances a great hurry to select claims; and the new comers had to travel over the country in the rainy season, in search of homes. Their animals being poor, they found it difficult to get along as fast as they desired. Many causes combined to make them unhappy for the time being. The long rainy seasons were new to them; and they preferred the snow and frozen ground to the rain and mud. There were no hotels in the country, as there was nothing wherewith to pay the bills. The old settlers had necessarily to throw open their doors to the new emigrants, and entertain them free of charge.

Our houses were small long cabins, and our bedding scarce. The usual mode of travel, was for each one to carry his blankets with him and sleep upon the puncheon floor. Our families were often overworked in waiting upon others, and our provisions vanished before the keen appetites of our new guests. They bred a famine wherever they went.[4]

There is a story, perhaps apocryphal, about one poor farmer who, because of his location on the main road south from Oregon City to the upper valley, was troubled by uninvited guests almost every night. In desperation the man determined one day to turn the traffic to his advantage and so hung a sign out of his home advertising it as an inn. From that day on he was never bothered by travelers. Daniel Waldo would have probably sympathized with this pioneer, for he also lived on the thoroughfare and was well-known for his hospitality. "I accomodated quite a number of people in my house out here on the road. We had not very many beds; they would sleep on the floor anyhow. I would give them their supper and breakfast. It was pretty hard on the women, but they were healthy."[5]

From these and similar comments we might too easily assume that the newcomers were only a burden to the frontier economy. In fact, quite the opposite was true. The livelihood of the established settlers depended upon agriculture, and yet, except for the Hudson's Bay Company, there was no ready market for their crops. Until the gold rush attracted thousands of miners, California usually supplied its own needs. The Russian-American and Sandwich Island markets were both of limited size and largely controlled by the British corporation. As long as there were only a few inefficient fur-trappers-turned-farmers growing wheat, there was no danger of overproduction, but with the rapid extension of cultivation increased harvests threatened to reduce the value of grain. Such a reduction would have proven fatal to the colony, for every pioneer farmer depended upon the sale of his surplus wheat to purchase those necessities he himself could not produce. A new market was absolutely necessary for the economic well-being of the colony, and the hungry immigrants provided it.

Unlike the Hudson's Bay Company and the Methodist stores at Fort Vancouver and Oregon City, the exhausted arrivals had neither money nor goods with which to pay the farmers for their wheat. They had only one thing of value: their ability to work. Some were hired as regular employees for set terms of service. Others became itinerant laborers and contracted for specific projects. Sometimes men banded together into informal crews which specialized in making such capital improvements as cabins or rail fences. John Bacon remembered his first job on the frontier making rails:

I came to Oregon City because that was the only place known. The first thing I did after landing—I landed Saturday night after dark—and on Sunday morning three of us got a job of making rails several miles from here. We took a job of making 5,000 rails . . . for a man by the name of Peter H. Hatch. His claim was about five miles from here up on the Clackamas. . . . The first 3 years I made rails all the time. I used to call myself a pretty good railmaker. We used to get $10 a thousand, a dollar a hundred and board. We would take pay in anything we could get. Most of us preferred horses or stock or something we could use. We preferred them to orders because we could not use them. At first of course I had to learn; I never had done anything of the kind. After I had got the hang of it, and a knowledge of how to pick out the timber, I used to average about 200 a day. Oftentimes I would make a great many more if I got good timber. We used the maul and wedge entirely.[6]

Often the workers were all members of one family, and their employment at the business lasted only for several months the first winter. Through their exertions during that time, they fed themselves and usually accumulated enough credit to finance the establishment of their own farm. Typical of this second and more numerous class was the Joseph Earl family, which crossed overland to Oregon in 1845 and in the spring of 1846 made one of the first settlements south of the Santiam River. William, the eldest son, headed his mother's family and as his younger brother Robert later reminisced, "we moved out on the thewlinton [Tualatin] plaines to winter among the French and halfbreeds . . . we made rails for grub and lived on dry peas the most of the time William Earl went to the upper end of the valey to see the country South of the Santam river what is known as Linn Co. he liked the country came back and in April we started for the new country . . . one of my brothers stoped in French prair to work for wheat for seed."[7]

Families that were bankrupted by the hardships of their overland journey and that lacked the assistance of more affluent relatives or friends often found temporary work insufficient for their needs. For these settlers a longer term of employment was necessary before they could afford to start new farms. At first, positions were limited almost entirely to those offered by the Hudson's Bay Company, but as the older districts were more densely settled and the number of towns grew, jobs became much more numerous. Contributing to this increase were the established farmers of French Prairie and the Tualatin Plains, who, after several prosperous years of selling wheat and other agricultural products, wished to retire from the active management of their claims by renting them to sharecroppers.

The extent of tenant farming in the Willamette Valley during the 1840s is difficult to ascertain. Although it may be safely assumed that sharecropping was relatively unimportant in the overall economy, scattered references in personal narratives and early newspapers indicate it was not uncommon, especially among new immigrants who had lost all their possessions. Agreements differed slightly from one property to another, but usually the shares appear to have been divided equally between owner and tenant. Allison Beers' tenant in the fall of 1845 was William Shaw, who got half of what he raised but had to board himself. That same year Alvin T. Smith's sharecropper arranged to receive both 50 percent of the crop and his board. In addition, he was provided with all the necessary seeds, animals, and tools.[8]

The importance of a barter economy in which labor was exchanged for agricultural products and other goods cannot be overestimated. To most new immigrants the strange prairies and woodlands of the Willamette Valley seemed to offer a meager quantity of native foods. Peter Burnett noted that,

For the first two years after our arrival, the great difficulty was to procure provisions. Had the country contained the same amount of wild game, wild fruits and honey as were found in the Western States at an early day our condition would have been better. But the only wild fruit we found was a variety of berries; such as blackberries; raspberries, strawberries, blueberries, cranberries and other varieties which we found not only abundant, but of most superior quality. We found only one nut in the country, and that was the hazel nut in small quantities. There were no wild grapes or plums, and no honey, wild or tame.[9]

Undoubtedly, Burnett's attitudes were conditioned by the fact that he lived on the Tualatin Plains, a fairly well-settled district that had been regularly hunted with firearms for more than thirty years. Not even his neighbor, the famous trapper Joseph Meek, could depend upon having meat in the larder. In the early years, and in less frequented districts to the south, the chances of killing wild game were probably better. Charles

Wilkes wrote in 1841, "We were informed that there are plenty of elk, and deer, and that the grizzly is also common. Wild ducks and geese are quite numerous in the spring and fall. . . ." Already by 1846, however, Lieutenant Neil Howison reported:

I was surprised to find so great a scarcity of game in the country. I lugged a heavy gun more than a hundred and fifty miles through the Wilhammette valley, and in all that ride saw but deer. Wolves are numerous, and prey upon other animals, so that the plains are entirely in their possession. The little venison I saw in Oregon was poor and insipid; a fat buck is a great rarity. Elk are still numerous, but very wild, living in the depths of the forests, or near those openings which the white man has not yet approached.[10]

Years of experience accumulated by missionaries and trappers indicated that significant numbers of settlers could not be supported by nature's bounty. Time and again letters sent east spoke of how in this respect the new country was quite different from the old and that "emigrants should go prepared to work and not to hunt."[11] Perhaps as a consequence of these admonitions few immigrants appear to have attempted living off the land. Useful native plants such as the camas were ignored more often than not. The Earls of Linn County, although they lived on the outermost edge of settlement, did not own even a single firearm.

Boiled wheat, potatoes, salted pork, and beef were the pioneers' principal foods. These four commodities together with labor became the primary items of exchange. Wheat, the main cash crop both for local consumption and export, was especially important, for in the absence of an official currency the provisional government made it Oregon's legal tender. The rate of exchange was officially fixed at one dollar per bushel, and merchants were required to accept it at that value.

The system's ultimate creditors were the merchants, who until the late 1840s located themselves almost exclusively at the Willamette Falls or Fort Vancouver. During this time the trade was dominated by two establishments, George Abernethy's store which succeeded the Methodists at Oregon City and, of course, the Hudson's Bay Company, which maintained outlets at both places. The latter firm was especially important, for by extending credit to hundreds of needy immigrants in 1843 and 1844 John McLoughlin created a sizable debtor class among the Americans.

The Hudson's Bay Company maintained the largest stock of quality merchandise at reasonable prices and so by preference attracted the greater portion of the normal trade. Merchandise in greatest demand included cloth, readymade clothing of all types, shoes, hardware, tools, and imported staples such as coffee, sugar, and salt. In return, the Hudson's Bay Company and its competitors could receive by choice any sort of trade—most commonly some kind of agricultural produce—or they could at least technically be required by law to accept wheat. Because of this legal stipulation merchants of necessity became wheat traders. To collect its extensive debts, the British firm was forced to maintain receiving warehouses at Champoeg and near the mouth of the Yamhill River. From these places the grain was brought down to the falls in boats for milling and export.

In most respects wheat was admirably suited for its primary role in frontier commerce. When stored properly it was essentially nonperishable. It could be cultivated, harvested, transported, and processed by crude methods. It could be measured exactly in any required amount, and its nutritional value made it relatively valuable for its bulk and weight. This last quality, while permitting its profitable shipment in large quantities, made wheat and every other common agricultural commodity too burdensome for everyday business transactions. In the barter economy of Oregon, this, plus the fact that it was difficult to enforce wheat's official status in most personal transactions, often made mutually agreeable exchanges between individuals nearly impossible. What one man offered was many times of no immediate value to another.

In attempting to overcome the difficulties created by the absence of an official currency, settlers often paid one another with promissory notes or personal notes drawn against their accounts at one of the stores. The system that evolved was one in which the farmer exchanged his wheat and other products several times a year for a particular merchant's goods, at the same time building a fund of extra credit from which he and his debtors could later draw. Everyone had to keep detailed records, and the shopkeepers who played the role of bankers had to be especially careful.

Strange as it may seem, with all the poverty and distress that existed, there appear to have been relatively few instances of fraud. The one notable exception was the apparent failure of many immigrants to repay the emergency loans made to them by Chief Factor McLoughlin. Even so, notes were of only restricted utility in alleviating the money shortage. Their most serious deficiency was that their real value varied from one merchant to the next depending upon the amount of stock each had at hand. Orders drawn against a small store having little, or no, merchandise were essentially valueless. Hence the ill repute enjoyed by "Abernethy Money," which often could be traded only at a significant discount. In marked contrast was "Ermatinger Money" named for Frank Ermatinger, the clerk charged with the management of the Hudson's Bay Company's store in Oregon City. Because of the great variety of high quality merchandise offered by this establishment, its orders were considered as good as cash. As the number of firms increased, so did the intricacies of commercial activity. Only with the entry into the economy of California gold and federal currency after 1848 was the problem finally solved.

One characteristic of the Oregon frontier emphasized by the development of the complex system of credits was that the economic relationship of one man to another was not so much one of independence as it was of interdependence. Settlers attempted to provide for as many of their own needs as possible, but true self-sufficiency was probably never attained or even tried. Certainly, most contemporary accounts indicate that the idea of ekeing out a bare subsistence on an isolated claim was anathema to the aspirations of the bulk of the rural population. Most immigrants looked upon the farm as one of the best means of successfully entering and participating in an expanding commerical economy.

For this reason, once their immediate needs for food and shelter had been satisfied and they had accumulated enough capital, the Americans began searching for that most basic element in an agricultural society—land. Many conditions affected their quest. As previously noted, the country's diverse physical environment led to a concentration of settlement in those areas perceived by the pioneers as most naturally suited for habitation, the forest boundaries. Then, too, the matter of distance and resulting transportation costs had to be carefully considered. If the prospective farmer wished to compete effectively in local markets, or in the export trade of agricultural produce, he had to weigh the quality of the available land against its distance from trade centers. Inasmuch as these were situated below

the falls and at Astoria, rural settlement gravitated toward the richer, more accessible areas of the lower Willamette Valley and the Clatsop Plains. Only after the first large migrations of the 1840s had populated the better prairie lands north of the Santiam River did the immigrants' attention begin to shift to the more distant southern districts. Even then, a contributing factor in their increased interest was the growth of a new market associated with traffic along the southern emigrant road after 1846.

Once the settler had viewed the countryside and chosen a particular area for his future home, the next task awaiting him was acquisition of title to his land. To obtain property, a person could either lay claim to a parcel of unoccupied territory or purchase the rights of an earlier claimant. Throughout the 1830s land was so plentiful and the population so small that real estate was seldom bought or traded. Preemption and use alone determined a man's right to hold land. This situation was largely a result of Oregon's unsettled political status which freed settlers from the restrictive land laws of either England or the United States.

As long as the bulk of the population was drawn from the ranks of the Hudson's Bay Company or the Methodist Mission, individual conscience, plus the extralegal influence of these two formidable organizations, ensured a proper respect for property. In the face of increasing independent immigration, however, so idyllic a situation could not last. By the fall of 1842, it had already become apparent that if the older inhabitants of the Willamette were to uphold their rights against interlopers, they would have to establish a formal legal code and an authority to sustain it. To this end, American settlers together with a few French Canadians organized an independent provisional government in the spring of 1843.

Among the new body's first actions was its adoption of an Organic Code based upon the laws of Iowa. Unlike the founders of the legal system of the latter territory, however, the authors of the Oregon statutes were not bound to respect the primacy of federal law. As a result, an opportunity existed to formulate legislation more beneficial to themselves than that current in the United States. David Hill, Robert Shortess, and William Doty were the members of the legislative committee concerned with land claims, and the law they presented for adoption seems to have owed much to unsuccessful bills introduced into the United States Senate in 1841 and 1842 by senators Lewis

Linn and Thomas Benton of Missouri. One of Linn's proposals which seems to have particularly struck the fancy of the committee and other Oregon settlers was that all male Caucasian inhabitants should receive 640 acres of free land. As finally enacted on July 5, 1843, the crucial section of the Organic Code consisted of only four articles:

ARTICLE 1. Any person now holding or hereafter wishing to establish a claim to land in this territory, shall designate the extent of his claim by natural boundaries, or by marks at the corners, and on the lines of such claim, and have the extent and boundaries of said claim recorded in the office of territorial recorder, in a book to be kept by him for that purpose, within twenty days from the time of making said claim. Provided, that those who shall already be in possession of land, shall be allowed one year from the passage of this act to file a description of his claim in the recorder's office.

ARTICLE 2. All claimants shall, within six months of the time of recording their claims, make permanent improvements upon the same by building or enclosing, and also become an occupant upon said claims within one year from the date of said record.

ARTICLE 3. No individual shall be allowed to hold a claim of more than one square mile, of 640 acres in a square or oblong farm, according to the natural situation of the premises; nor shall any individual be allowed to hold more than one claim at the same time. Any person complying with the provisions of these ordinances, shall be entitled to the same recourse against trespass as in other cases by law provided.

ARTICLE 4. No person shall be entitled to hold such a claim upon city or town sites, extensive water privileges, or other situations necessary for the transaction of mercantile or manufacturing operations, and to the detriment of the community—Provided, that nothing in these laws shall be so construed to affect any claim of any mission of a religious character, made previous to this time, of an extent not more than six miles square.[12]

The legal basis of property ownership in Oregon had been established. To avoid future litigation and economic hardship each claimant was technically required to survey, mark, and record his boundaries. At the same time, large scale speculation was hindered by residence and improvement requirements and the restriction on the amount of land any individual could hold. The act was not without bias, for while established settlers had one year to record their claims, new applicants were granted only twenty days. Also, the preferential consideration shown the missions under article 4 contrasted sharply with the abrogation of John McLoughlin's Oregon City claim.

The initial land law of the new government stood for only one year before men of the 1843 migration, troubled by the twenty day registration provision, replaced it with a more equitable and comprehensive act. Passed on June 25, 1844, the second "Act in Relation to Land Claims" became, with only minor amendments, the legal basis of all titles and all real estate transactions made during the next six years.

An Act in Relation to Land Claims

SECTION 1. Be it enacted by the Legislative Committee of Oregon, as follows, That all persons who have heretofore made, or shall hereafter make, permanent improvements upon a place, with a bonafide intention of occupying and holding the same for himself, and shall continue to occupy and cultivate the same, shall be entitled to hold six hundred and forty acres, and shall hold only one claim at the same time, *provided*, a man may hold town lots in addition to his claim.

SECTION 2. That all claims hereafter made shall be in a square form, if the nature of the ground shall permit; and in case the situation will not permit, shall be in an oblong form.

SECTION 3. That in all cases where claims are already made, and in all cases where there are agreed lines between the parties occupying adjoining tracts, such claims shall be valid to the extent of six hundred and forty acres, although not in a square or oblong form.

SECTION 4. That in all cases where claims shall hereafter be made, such permanent improvements shall be made within two months from the time of taking up said claim, and the first settler or his successor shall be deemed to hold the prior right.

SECTION 5. That no person shall hold a claim under the provisions of the act except free males, over the age of eighteen, who would be entitled to vote if of lawful age, and widows; *provided*, no married man shall be debarred from holding a claim under this act because he is under the age of eighteen.

SECTION 6. That all laws heretofore passed in regard to land claims be and the same are hereby repealed.

SECTION 7. That all persons complying with the provisions of this act shall be deemed in possession to the extent of six hundred and forty acres, or less, as the case may be and shall have the remedy of forcible entry and detainer against intruders, and the action of trespass against trespassers.[13]

Added to this land law on December 24, 1844, was "An Act to Amend and Explain the Act upon Land Claims, Passed at the Last June Session of This House."

SECTION 1. Be it enacted by the Legislative Committee of Oregon, as follows, that the word "occupancy" in said act, shall be so construed as to require the claimant to either personally reside upon his claim himself, or to occupy the same by the personal residence of his tenant.

SECTION 2. That any person shall be authorized to take six hundred acres of his claim in the prairie, and forty acres in the timber, and such parts of his claim need not be adjoining to each other.

SECTION 3. That where two persons take up their claims jointly, not exceeding twelve hundred and eighty acres, they may hold the same jointly for the term of one year by making the improvements required by said act upon any part of said claim, and may hold the same longer than one year if they make said improvements within the year upon each six hundred and forty acres.[14]

Although the initial land law was repealed, certain key provisions were incorporated into the new statute to protect against land frauds. The limitation of ownership to only one claim of 640 acres and the maintenance of existing boundaries were sustained, as were the requirements of property improvements and actual residence. In the latter stipulations, however, significant modifications were made. The old land law allowed claimants a full half year's grace before requiring improvements to their property. The new one gave only two months, making it more difficult to "lock up" virgin land by the mere laying out of boundaries.

Changes made in the occupancy requirement reflected the new economic forces unleashed by the newcomers. Whereas the original statute had assumed that claimants and occupants were synonomous, its successor recognized for the first time the existence of tenancy on the frontier and hence, indirectly, the increased scarcity and speculative value of land. In clarifying the peculiar legal positions of both claimant and investor, the law maintained the superiority of the farmer's right. By doing so, it established a legal basis for absentee ownership. Possession of unoccupied land was also extended to include town lots. These were not counted against the acreage limitations of an individual's claim, and they became a primary factor in land speculation related to urbanization along the lower Willamette River.

Hardly less important than the clarification of occupancy was the matter of title transfer. Both land laws remained strangely silent on this subject. The only allusion made in either document was found in section 4 of the 1844 statute, which stated that "the first settler or his successor shall be deemed to hold the prior right." As generally interpreted by the settlers, absence of explicit regulations at least technically forbade land sales. At the same time, the increased demand for farmland with each year's migration drove up property values and with them created the opportunity for profitable speculation.

When the frontier's first newspaper, the *Oregon Spectator,* began publishing in early 1846, real estate sales had already become commonplace. Among the properties advertised through the press were B. Delcour's claim on French Prairie, including log buildings and about two hundred acres of enclosed land; the A. Cook claim on the Tualatin Plains, which had eighty acres in cultivation with a good fence, a log cabin, and timber for a framed dwelling and barn; and the Richard Gwen property, also on the Tualatin Plains, which had eighty well-fenced acres, three comfortable log cabins, and a double barn.

Although land sales occurred frequently a more common subversion of the law consisted of selling only the improvements, which were, of course, inseparable from the land. One participant in this business remembered:

We would go on to a piece of land and set out stakes, calculating and setting off a section or a mile square. We would make marks; and of course if we wanted to leave our claims and others wanted to take possession we would sell our improvements; we could not sell the land. I changed my claim and when I sold it I sold my improvements for $1,000. That was in 1849 after the gold discovery in California. My improvements consisted of a house, barn, and fencing.[15]

No precise figure can be given regarding the number of such real estate transactions made between 1843 and the end of the decade, but from all accounts the amount was not inconsiderable. A purely subjective estimate based upon a survey of family histories and manuscript materials is that perhaps as much as a quarter or a third of the immigrant farmers purchased their claims rather than take up virgin land. By 1847, activity had increased to the point that the *Oregon Spectator* was warning new immigrants, "you will find the same disposition for speculation in land claims that you may have found at an earlier period in some of the new territory of the Mississippi valley . . . also beware of town speculators."[16]

Although petty land agents were not thwarted by legal strictures, the activities of those with grander schemes seem to have been severely limited. Restricted partnerships were allowed, but the special thirty-six square mile dispensation granted the missionaries in 1843 was struck down. Still, many of the meaner aspects of title acquisition and maintenance familiar to men from the western states persisted. Settlers' property rights were challenged by intruders, and claim jumping became an increasingly common affair. During his first ten years of residence on the Tualatin Plains, Alvin T. Smith had to warn off trespassers on two separate occasions. So serious did the problem become on the plains that his neighbors on at least one occasion gathered at the Methodist meeting house for an anti-claim-jumping meeting.

In the absence of effective governmental control, family clans or loosely structured protective associations offered their members perhaps the best possible protection. If a problem between two parties was not settled satisfactorily through arbitration, the established community usually stood ready to intervene in behalf of the first settler. As provided by section 7 of the land law, the aggrieved could forcibly enter a residence and hold trespassers for prosecution. More than any other factor it was probably this ever present threat of legalized violence and social ostracism that brought some measure of order to land acquisition in the more highly valued and densely settled northern districts.

Considering the limited size of the population and the tremendous amount of unoccupied land, the struggle for a particular site might at first glance seem to have been needless. Well into the next decade, extensive areas remained unsettled—even on the Tualatin Plains and French Prairie. Part of the claim-jumping problem can be traced to the relatively large size of the claims, which collectively included much of the vital forest-prairie boundary. Most immigrants were used to farms with less than half the acreage allowed in Oregon, and it was difficult for some to accept the right of early residents to claim so much land. Then, too, hardly any of the existing claims even approached full development. Usually the enclosed and cultivated ground included but a small portion of the properties, and large parcels of the best land were utilized only for the pasturage of livestock.

Another source of irritation to the new arrivals was that much of this seemingly open, but legally private, property had not been properly surveyed or marked. Although required to do so by law, most settlers did not undertake even this most elementary task until a dispute arose. It is little wonder that hard feelings developed on both sides. For more than a few the most frustrating tasks encountered in establishing a farm were the first—the acquisition of capital for food, tools, clothing, and the securing of a reasonably clear title to land.

CHAPTER 7

The Farm and Rural Economy

THE REAL LABORS of settlement began once the immigrants had recovered sufficiently from the rigors of their overland journey to move up valley and had obtained a parcel of land. Having already procured at least a temporary supply of food from some merchant or farmer, the first task confronting them was the provision of immediate shelter. Whenever possible they found lodgings in the home of a nearby relative or friend. Lacking such connections they sometimes resorted to local schools or meeting houses. For the Peter Burnett family, home was a place of worship. "By permission of a neighbor of ours, a sincere minister, we were allowed to occupy temporarily, the log cabin used for a church; upon condition that I would permit him to have services there every Sunday."[1] Since public buildings were not at all common, the only alternative to a neighbor's house was usually an open camp.

One early pioneer who lived in such a bivouac was Alvin T. Smith, a layman farmer attached to the Congregational mission in eastern Oregon, who after spending a futile year in the interior descended the Columbia River late in the summer of 1841 and settled on the Tualatin Plains. Unlike most of his contemporaries, Smith kept a diary of his daily activities, a journal concerned not so much with personalities as with the everyday management of a wilderness farm. The insights it gives to problems facing the frontiersmen are numerous, but its special value lies in its development of a sense of time and perspective lost in other descriptions of pioneer life. It is both the plan and the timetable of a typical farm's growth.

As with most immigrants who opened unimproved claims, the first major task facing Smith was the erection of a permanent dwelling. On the frontier where sawed lumber was scarce and expensive until the 1850s this meant building a log cabin. No detailed description of the home has survived. From other sources it is apparent that a number of architectural styles were common in Oregon, and which he might have chosen is impossible to determine. Double cabins were sometimes built, and hewn timber construction was also occasionally used. If it was like most, however, the house was probably a single room affair made from unhewn fir logs with a shake roof of split cedar.

Although a simple structure, the cabin's construction was no easy matter, even for so experienced a mechanic as Smith. Before work could begin, helves had to be made for the axes. Then too, a vehicle of some sort was needed to transport the larger logs from forest to building site. Usually crude wheels or "trucks" were made by simply sawing off sections of a log and cutting a hole in the center for an axle. The screaming noise that these contrivances made under a heavy load was ear-splitting and could be heard for miles. Smith finished his wheels in one day and began cutting and hauling split boards and logs. Only after two weeks of exhausting effort, however, had sufficient materials been accumulated for raising the house.

Even with the walls erected, much work remained. More than sixty work days were needed to complete the basic carpentry involved in building a shake roof, puncheon floor, attic, door, and window. All were time-consuming tasks made more difficult by the absence of adequate tools and metal hardware. Without nails, Smith and his neighbors were forced to resort to intricate mortise-tenon construction and the use of withes, pliable "hazel" switches which substituted for rope or wire in binding together the roof, door, and shutters. Lack of easily quarried rock also presented construction problems, for without it fireplaces had to be made of earth. Smith waited until the fall when he was able to make sunbaked adobe bricks. Others built hearths of tamped mud or wattle and daub.

Interiors were usually furnished in spartan style, for little furniture survived the overland journey. Used pieces were already shipped from the East Coast around Cape Horn in the 1840s, but supplies were limited and prices relatively high. As a result, beds, chairs, tables, and most other furnishings were homemade. Alvin Smith built a bedstead, table, and undoubtedly many other items. Describing similar frontier cabins, William Strong later recalled, "they had a table generally made of stakes put in the ground and shakes put on top; they never required moving; bedsteads were stakes in the ground and slats bound together with rawhide."[2] A more prosperous family might have had a single rocking chair, a cupboard, or some other family treasure, but seldom did it have anything else.

Once the new house had been made habitable, the pioneer's attention shifted to cultivation and agricultural improvements. In the early spring, a dooryard garden was planted to supply the household with fresh vegetables. According to Lincoln Wilkes, whose family lived north of Smith on the northern edge of the Tualatin Plains, the most common vegetables grown in his locale were potatoes, cabbages, peas, turnips, onions, parsnips, tomatoes, and carrots. Corn was grown only for roasting ears, and string beans were dried for winter use. Besides these food crops most farmers raised their own tobacco and grew chicory as a coffee substitute.

Beyond the garden's small picketed enclosure stretched the open prairie made green by approaching spring. Breaking the grassland usually began in March, when the weather had begun to improve and the ground was still wet. The plow was a crude affair, fashioned from either hand-hewn wood or just a twisted piece of oak. Most often the plowshare was the only part made of iron, although sometimes no metal was used at all. One or two yoke of oxen provided motive power, and with a little experience and luck a farmer could plow two acres of new land each day. Alvin Smith began plowing on March 16, and continued intermittently until May 13, laboring approximately fifteen days at the task. It is not known exactly how much acreage he opened that first season, but the amount was probably less than the sixteen acres he cultivated the following year. Most accounts suggest this was not an unusually small quantity. Peter Burnett sowed only three acres in wheat his first year on the Tualatin Plains, and the large Earl family of Linn County plowed only twenty acres for both field and garden. The 1850 census of agriculture indicates that even after several years residence most farmers had "improved" less than eighty acres of their claims.

Several factors accounted for the small acreages initially cultivated by the pioneer farmers. From a strictly technological standpoint the plows were inefficient and easily broken. Also, they were drawn almost exclusively by oxen, the same animals that had recently hauled the immigrants' wagons across the continent. After the long journey and the rigors of a winter spent in the open, many of these beasts were so weakened that they were incapable of performing heavy labor for extended periods of time. Still another element was the limited amount of wheat available for planting. In an economy where many persons lived on the verge of starvation, only so much seed could be saved. For impoverished newcomers this was especially true, and it was only by the strictest conservation that even fifteen or twenty bushels of this vital resource remained for planting the first crop.

If these difficulties were not enough to limit the first year's effort, insufficient time usually was. Many jobs vital to the support of a family and the establishment of a new farm demanded the pioneer's attention. After the erection of the house and the cultivation attendant to the sowing of the gardening and fields, no task demanded so much effort as fencing the plowed ground. Following the custom of the western frontier, livestock was normally allowed to wander freely about the countryside. To protect his crops each farmer had to enclose his fields with a sturdy fence. On the Tualatin Plains, as throughout the rest of Oregon, "the pioneer's field fences were all built of rails, laid worm fashion. In this valley the most common method of strengthening the fence was by laying a pole on top, wherever it crossed a panel, a stake was leaned into the angle, two stakes to each panel of the fence."[3]

According to the act defining lawful fences passed by the territorial legislature in 1852, Virginia worm fences had to be "sufficiently staked and ridered, or locked at each joint, five feet in height" to enjoy the protection of the law. On rare occasions fences were built stake and rider fashion. This style made a strong enclosure while it lasted, but the stakes usually rotted within several years. In addition to the field enclosures the pioneers often erected split picket fences around their homes and gardens. Although these were supposed to be chicken proof, the birds usually found some way of getting across.

Alvin Smith built both worm and picket fences soon after planting his crops. Sixteen days were required for splitting, hauling, and laying up rails around the wheat field. The dooryard fence took another three days. Twenty-two days were spent building and repairing fences that first year, and subsequently he worked nineteen days (1843) and three and one half days (1844). In the fall of this last year, however, a claim jumper attempted to take control of a portion of the farm. To protect it from future incursions, Smith spent more than fifty days during the next year fencing the greater part of his property.[4]

Once the fences had been completed, other major improvements normally awaited conclusion of the first harvest. In the meanwhile, farmers divided their time between such minor jobs as constructing watering troughs or pig pens and preparing their tools. A cradle for cutting wheat and a rake for gathering it had to be made, the grindstone hung, and a threshing floor prepared. To bring in the grain in August, Smith had to build a new cart. To clean it during September and October he made a riddle. Not until the next year's food supply had been assured did the improvement of the farm begin again.

One of the larger projects demanding the attention of progressive farmers was the provision of some rudimentary protection for livestock and harvested crops. Because the Oregon winters were normally mild compared to those of the Middle West, many farmers were tempted to let their animals fend for themselves. Sometimes they paid heavily for this lack of foresight. During the winter of 1846–47, for instance, the editor of the *Oregon Spectator* noted that because of snow, "some have lost upwards of 20 head of cattle, and others something under that number; . . . the hogs have been obliged to seek shelter in the woods, and the six or seven days of cold weather which we have had, took away many of them."[5]

Even more destructive to unprotected livestock were predators that attacked calves, horses, and other farm animals. Among the more fearsome killers were cougars. According to contemporary reports, they were both numerous and unusually bold, often entering farmyards to kill. During his travels through the settlements in 1841, Charles Wilkes noted they were one of the more serious deterents to successful ranching on French Prairie. In a humorous anecdote concerning the settlement of Linn County, Robert Earl recounted how his brother, William, "heard the hogs sqeling about 200 years from the house he jumped out of bed without any pants on and ran down there he never kept a gun on the ranch when he got there he found a cogar hold of a hog he scared him loose he acted like [he] wanted a man for Super."[6]

On rare occasions bears also troubled the livestock. When Sydney Moss first met Joseph Meek out on the Tualatin Plains, "he was building a pig stye. He had got a few pigs and the bears were very troublesome and were killing them."[7] A much greater plague than both bears or cougars combined were the wolves and coyotes that thrived on the growing herds of every district. Of the wolves' ravages on the Clatsop Plains, Mrs. Martha Minto observed, "we had brought through a valuable mare and stallion colt, the latter was destroyed by a band of wolves near the house . . . the wolves also destroyed our hogs, notwithstanding our screams and shouts—our calves had to be kept in a corral built close against the house, and almost into it."[8] On three different occasions wolves killed young animals belonging to Alvin Smith, and near Salem, beginning in 1844, Thomas Kaiser was forced to corral his mares and colts for about five years to preserve them. When Daniel Waldo first arrived in Marion County, "the wolves ate up lots of horses. They ate up 14 for our company one spring. Cattle would fight them, but horses would run; the wolves would run them. I got some nux vomica that killed them off in about two months. We just rubbed it on a file and put it on a piece of meat."[9]

To protect their animals from the dangers of the wilderness and of winter, the better farmers built sheds and barns of unhewn logs. Since barns were much larger and more difficult to build than cabins their construction only began once the farmer's more rudimentary needs had been satisfied. Alvin Smith started the project on December 21, 1842, slightly more than a year after his first settlement. As with the house, logs had to be cut and hauled to the site with oxen. Altogether this first step required twenty-six working days and was completed only on the first of July, 1843. Preparations for raising the structure consumed an additional twenty-one days. First, a trace of the barn's outer walls had to be laid out on the ground and the foundation leveled. Then structural timbers were sawed manually with the aid of a hired neighbor while the normal operations of the farm continued apace. Finally, on August 24, neighbors were called and the barn raising began. The task was a formidable one and took four days, the last log being lifted on September 5, 1843.[10]

As with the house, the raising of the barn walls signified just the beginning of the carpentry phase of construction. Four men were employed to assist in making shakes, putting up rafters, and covering over the roof. This took forty-two working days, but once the roof was completed it protected the interior so that work could continue through the winter on the last sizable task, the laying of a floor made from sawed lumber. Since he allotted time to other necessary business, the work progressed slowly. Not until May 24, 1844, more than 140 work days after he had cut his first logs, did Alvin Smith finish his barn. Other buildings besides the barn were put up, but none were much more than small sheds in comparison. In November 1844, a potato cellar was finished. In December 1845, a sturdy pig house was built, and in the fall of 1848 a cowshed was completed.

Besides the major projects, a multitude of necessary, yet less noteworthy, occupations demanded constant attention. The daily chores, cutting firewood, milking, and hauling water for the house, always waited, and there were the fields and animals to manage. It was not enough to merely plow, sow, and reap. Vigilance was necessary to protect the maturing crops from predators. Each spring Alvin Smith spent long days keeping crows from his corn. So troublesome were the winged bandits, that tree bark had to be strung up about the field to frighten them off when no one was around. Then there were the hogs. Livestock of all sorts attempted to break down fences and eat the crops, but none was so persistent or distressingly successful as this adaptable animal. Cows and horses could be easily discouraged by a sturdy rail barrier, whereas swine treated the impediment more as a challenge than as an insurmountable obstacle. Only determined watchfulness and prompt replacement of damaged rails thwarted their efforts to break into the fields.

At times it must have appeared to the settlers that their foraging animals were consciously attempting to exert their independence. Whenever or wherever their presence was unwelcome, then and there they could be found. As long as they were unwanted they were everywhere in the way, but let some need of them arise and they became conspicuous by their absence. The open pasture-lands of the countryside provided stock with infinite opportunity for independent adventure. In the broken prairies and forest, stray animals were soon lost from view. Each year settlers wasted many days, even weeks, searching for their livestock. Often they were never recovered. Some animals wandered away from their neighborhoods and were claimed by unknown settlers. Others reverted to an almost feral condition and attached themselves to wild bands which frequented the margins of settlement. On the open prairies of the south, there were herds of wild horses and cattle, and in the northern districts aggressive gangs of pigs haunted the woodlands.

Conscientious farmers spent many days each year working with the livestock that did not escape. To increase the size and improve the quality of their herds, the more progressive pioneers attempted to selectively herd their animals with the neighborhood's better stock. Alvin Smith borrowed Joseph Gale's old ram for his ewes and used Charles McKay's English boar to inseminate his sows. The use of some particularly favored bull by several neighbors was a common practice which at least partially offset the genetically detrimental effects of grazing animals of varying quality on the unenclosed pastures.

Slaughtering the animals was another chore the complexity of which is today too often overlooked. The greatest difficulty was preserving the meat, for without refrigeration fresh meat spoiled rapidly. When a larger animal was killed its carcass was usually divided among several neighbors or was salt cured. Curing solved the spoilage problem, but it also introduced new difficulties. Salt could only be obtained through trade, so the farmer had to be able to participate successfully in the greater economy of the frontier. In addition, the curing process required wooden casks. Of course, these also could be purchased, but more often than not the newer and less financially secure settlers did their own cooperage—another in an unending list of skills that were required to operate a farm.

Although contemporary accounts indicate that the settlers expended the greater portion of their energies on the completion of capital improvements and daily activities directly related to the maintenance of their properties, they also repeatedly stress that the internal operation of the farm was only one of several aspects of the economy which demanded the farmer's attention. Another was the establishment of formal commercial relations with town merchants, who would supply goods in exchange for agricultural produce.

A third and equally important matter to the Oregon pioneer was his commercial dealings with neighbors. Unfortunately, in most analyses of frontier economies little account has been taken of transactions made within local farm communities. If considered at all, they have been relegated to a position of economic insignificance. This is perhaps due to two erroneous premises commonly held by many modern investigators. The first of these is that the importance of trade can be accurately measured by the dollar value of currency and goods exchanged. The second is the patently false assumption that individual farms were so much alike in their needs and productions that there was little basis for economic interaction.

Error results in both cases from a failure to recognize the fundamental importance of labor as a medium of exchange—not only between the recently arrived indigent immigrants and the established community, but also between the various members of that same community. One cause of the confusion is that often there was no exchange of labor for goods, but rather a trade of labor for labor in turn. In the rudimentary technology of the frontier where sophisticated machinery was seldom available, it was often necessary to concentrate manual labor in quantities sufficient to perform large or difficult tasks. An individual could with some difficulty cut and haul logs for a building. Without assistance of his neighbors, however, the logs could not be lifted into place to form the walls. Other chores such as harvesting and fencing could be accomplished alone, but were most efficiently completed by a group.

A situation therefore existed in which each individual had a need for labor and at the same time could work for others. Temporary labor pools became an important element in financial transactions, making possible major capital improvements. Perhaps as much as any other necessity, this need for accessible labor bound farmers together in an economy of mutual interdependence and led to the development of distinct rural communities rather than to the creation of isolated and independent farmsteads.

Direct exchange of labor is so foreign to those of us who live in a money dominated economy that we often ascribe to it something other than an economic motive. How often we have heard about or have perhaps ourselves extolled the "wonderful frontier spirit of giving and community" that, so we are told, once transcended the meaner behavior of mortal men. Somehow when poverty was common and currency was scarce people were more virtuous, more caring, more cooperative. Friendly neighbors would gather together to raise a log cabin. The women held their quilting bees, and the men gladly helped one another in the fields.

Manuscripts do seem to indicate that cooperative enterprise was more common on the early frontier than it is today, but this was a cooperation born more of economic necessity than of ethical considerations. Normally, labor was not freely exchanged between neighbors. Instead, it was strictly accounted for by all parties concerned. If a man needed a specific item such as an axe, he bartered his own goods or labor in exchange. If he needed labor to help put up his barn, he did likewise.

The complexity and importance of this intracommunity economic activity should not be underestimated. For most settlers it was more time-consuming and more vital to daily life than the business they did with town merchants. Within the rural districts there always existed a need for specialized services and men who could perform them. Often individuals who had been apprenticed or informally educated in the rudiments of a trade in their youth served the communities' needs. Limited local markets and the primitive nature of the economy made it impractical for such men to rely solely on their business for a livelihood. Instead, they practiced their trades whenever possible as a useful addition to their agricultural incomes. By doing so they lost their identity as part-time tradesmen and were classified in official censuses simply as farmers. Yet, submerged within this seemingly homogeneous occupational class there existed the technological and professional expertise needed for economic survival. Many of the most fundamental economic transactions occurred between farmers. George Ebbert, the farmer, was also George Ebbert, blacksmith. Mr. Coates was a community cobbler, Payton Wilkes a tanner, Samuel Gilmore a sawyer, John Griffin and Harvey Clark preachers, and Joseph Gale a miller. Almost everyone had a second occupation—even Alvin Smith and his wife, who boarded and educated neighborhood children in their home.

Secondary occupations, intracommunity trade, labor pooling, extracommunity commerce, daily chores, farm development—these claimed most of the pioneers' time. All had to be attended to if the land was to be settled. All were necessary for survival. Together they formed a framework within which commercial relations between men were established and a viable economy developed. Ultimately they bound individuals to their neighbors in almost semiautonomous rural communities that, except for a limited commerce with town merchants in import goods and agricultural exports, had relatively few external economic contacts. Abominable roads, uncertain shipping schedules, and distant markets hardly affected them, for their very existence was, in fact, partially a response to these conditions.

CHAPTER 8

Frontier Agriculture

IN THE YEARS following the great migration of 1843, agriculture became the foundation of Oregon's frontier economy. Plows broke the land, and flower-covered prairies were transformed into patchworks of brown and green. Herds of cattle replaced the wild animals of an earlier period.

The identity of the first real farmer south of the Columbia River is uncertain. By the second decade of the nineteenth century domesticated livestock and crops had already been introduced by the Astorians and the North West Company. Agriculture languished, however, until the fur trade passed into the hands of the Hudson's Bay Company in 1821. Upon merger, new personnel were assigned to superintend existing operations on the coast and at the same time make them more profitable. Foremost among these men was Chief Factor John McLoughlin, who under Governor George Simpson's direction established a new headquarters on the north side of the Columbia upstream from the mouth of the Willamette River. As McLoughlin later recalled:

We came to the determination to abandon Astoria and go to Fort Vancouver, as it was a place where we could cultivate the soil and raise our own provisions. In March, 1825, we moved there, and that spring planted potatoes and sowed two bushels of peas, the only grain we had, and all we had. In the fall, I received from York Factory, a bushel of spring wheat, one bushel of oats, one bushel of Indian corn, for which the ground was too poor and the nights rather cool . . . as the farmers could not cultivate the ground without cattle, and as the Hudson Bay Company had only twenty-seven head, big and small, and as I saw at the time, no possibility of getting cattle by sea, and that was too expensive. I determined that no cattle should be killed at Vancouver, except one bull calf every year for revvet to make cheese.[1]

By such strict conservation of resources, and the expenditure of much effort, agriculture prospered and assumed an ever greater role in the Company's business. The harvest of 1834 yielded three thousand bushels of peas, four thousand bushels of wheat, one thousand of oats, and one thousand of barley, and by early 1835 the cattle herd had increased to about six hundred head. From McLoughlin's own calculation of twenty bushels of wheat per acre it would appear that this crop alone accounted for about two hundred acres of cultivated ground.

Under McLoughlin's direction, agriculture spread to the company's inland stations and southward with retired employees into the French Prairie settlement. During the 1830s farms were also begun by Nathaniel Wyeth and the Methodist missionaries. With few exceptions most of the attempts prospered. Development, however, was slow due to a number of retarding factors. The most serious was the scarcity of cattle, almost all of which were loaned from the Fort Vancouver herd and not for sale. This proved particularly vexing to some of the Americans, who recognized the potential for an extensive ranching economy in the great prairies of the upper Willamette Valley. Because of the normally mild winter climate cattle could graze unprotected in all seasons, and with little effort and several animals a man might soon become wealthy by frontier standards.

Through the influence and assistance of William A. Slacum, an official representative of the United States Department of State, individual settlers, together with the Hudson's Bay Company and the Methodist Mission, raised several thousand dollars for the importation of cattle into Oregon. A company of eleven men under the leadership of Ewing Young sailed to California in the spring of 1837, and there purchased approximately seven hundred cattle from Mexican authorities at Sonoma for three dollars per head. Six hundred and thirty of the original herd survived the journey to Oregon, and these were distributed among the subscribers according to the amount of money each had invested. Subsequently other herds were trailed northward to further increase the livestock population. Longhorned Spanish cattle wandered freely over the grasslands, and the valley began to earn a reputation as great stock country.

As the number of cattle increased during the late 1830s and early 1840s, ranching became an important element of the rural economy. East of the Willamette River, the Methodist herd, grown to over a thousand head, grazed along Mill Creek and on the hills south of Salem. West of the river, the Chehalem Valley and the prairies on either side of the Yamhill sustained even more livestock. In most cases the owners were immigrants like Ewing Young or George Gay, who had helped obtain animals from California.

In many respects the industry was remarkably similar to that of the Spanish Southwest. Throughout most of the year the black cattle roamed at will. Without care or need of winter feeding they ran half wild, a terror to anyone afoot. Once or twice a year riders brought all the animals of a neighborhood together for branding. On January 15, 1845, James Clyman described one such roundup.

I now witnessed the catching and branding of a lot of wild cattle about 500 ware drove in to a strong pound and 4 or 5 men well mount rode in to the pound   the animal to be taken being pointed out some one went full speed amongst the herd and threw a rope with a almost dead certainty a round the horns or neck of the animal the cord being made fast to his saddle Bow he stoped his horse and checked the speed of the animal and if his horse was not sufficiently strong 3, 4, or five other men threw their cords on the animal then putting spurs to their horses they draged him out of the pound by main force and hampering his legs with cords they threw him then Butchered or branded him as the case might be

From information I found that in this settlement caled Yam Hill their was owned and runing in the hills about two thousand head of wild cattle and about as many called tame which tameness consists in thir being able to ride amongst them and drive them conveniently nearly whare you wish the main bulk of these cattle are owned by Five individuals the other settlers being wrthless citizens or late imigrants which have but small stocks of Ten Twenty or thirty head[2]

In the same area in May 1845 he again reported:

to day commences the greate collection of wild cattle for the purpose of Branding and delivering all that have been sold or Traded for the last six months.

went to Mr. Jays (George Gay) to see the branding and marketing of wild cattle saw a pound full containing some 5 or 600 Head and 10 or 12 men on horse back Lassing and draging out by the saddle.

As settlement increased most of the larger herds of longhorns were divided and sold to new immigrants or were moved southward to the more extensive and uninhabited grasslands. By 1850, the only large herd remaining on the west side contained approximately 550 head and was under the care of Washington Riggs at the south end of the valley (map 33). In the north, the lower Yamhill remained an important cattle area, but the herds were moderate-sized. The three largest had between 250 and 300 head each and belonged to Glenn O. Burnett (Salt Creek), Pleasant Armstrong (South Fork), and Henry Cooper (North Fork). On the Tualatin Plains, Walter Pomeroy ran about 300 animals, and along the Rickreall Creek, Jesse Roberts kept 350 more.

The only great herd on the frontier was owned by Hamilton Campbell, a former member of the Methodist Mission. When this venerable institution was dissolved and its assets sold in 1844, "Cow" Campbell arranged to take over the entire mission herd on long-term credit. Although his ranch was located on the north bank of the lower Santiam River, his Spanish cattle roamed the entire country south from Salem into Linn County. Officially, the 1850 census credits him with twelve hundred animals, but no one knew exactly how many wild longhorns he really owned.

James Clyman, and other contemporary observers, continually emphasized the importance of large herds. Yet when computed from the agricultural census of 1850, the average herd of beef cattle appears to have contained only about sixteen animals. Of the almost twelve hundred cattle-owning households enumerated, only one dozen possessed more than a hundred head. Slightly more than one third owned fewer than five cattle, and 65 percent had less than ten.

One aspect of the cattle question which cannot be investigated through the census is quality. All sources indicate that the bloodlines of the original herds were entirely Spanish. For some time it has been fashionable to deprecate the qualities of these first importations, but in many regards they were especially well suited to the Oregon frontier. Their willingness and ability to fend for themselves was particularly useful to men who had many other obligations to contend with. Not the least of their advantages were their long, sharp horns and aggressive spirit. Predators which attacked other livestock with impunity had much more trouble with these combative creatures. Moreover, when pastured on the fine grasslands of the Willamette Valley, they attained moderate weight and made excellent beef.

The one serious drawback of the Spanish breed was that the cows produced notoriously little milk.

Just how little is indicated by Sir George Simpson's report that at the Hudson's Bay Company's dairy on Sauvie Island about one hundred milch cows yielded a yearly average of not more than sixty pounds of butter each. As a result, early settlers writing letters home recommended that immigrants should bring with them as many cattle of good stock as they could conveniently manage.

Significant alterations in the genetic characteristics of the herds began after 1843. That year the "Great Emigration" brought a thousand or more head of loose cattle into the valley. Among the largest herds were those of the Waldo and Applegate families—neither of which originally included more than about one hundred animals. This number seems to have been about all that a large and fairly wealthy family could manage. Most witnesses agreed that the usual quantity per household was much smaller.

A fairly typical example of the ratio of immigrants to livestock in a wagon train is given in a letter written by Cornelius Gilliam and reprinted in Bancroft's *History of Oregon.* According to Gilliam, his section of the 1844 migration contained 323 persons in seventy-two wagons with 160 cows, 143 young cattle, 410 oxen, 54 horses, and 41 mules.[3] That is, the number of range cattle roughly equaled that of the people. If, as other accounts suggest, this ratio was more or less maintained throughout the decade, the total quantity of breeding stock introduced probably did not exceed eight or ten thousand. Allowing for natural increase and the Spanish element, this estimate seems to correspond fairly well with the 1850 census figure of 28,907 milch and beef cattle.

Among the American imports, quality varied considerably from one herd to the next. Most of the cattle were Shorthorns, and Durhams apparently dominated the ranks of the better animals. The demand for blooded stock was great. Daniel Waldo reported that his were worth one hundred dollars apiece during the first years when longhorns could be had for nine dollars.

Ostensibly the most important reason for importing American cattle was the improvement of milking qualities. Comparison of butter and cheese yields with   number of milch cows, however, indicates th   perhaps the gains were not so great as migh   nave been expected. A representative sample of Benton County herds, for instance, shows butter production averaged less than fifty pounds per animal each year. Two Benton farmers, Nicholas Ownsbee and Benjamin

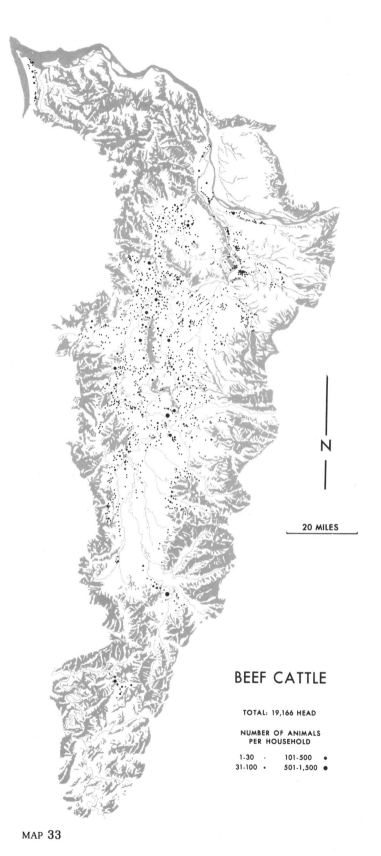

MAP 33

BEEF CATTLE

TOTAL: 19,166 HEAD

NUMBER OF ANIMALS
PER HOUSEHOLD

1-30   ·   101-500   •
31-100 ·   501-1,500 ●

N

20 MILES

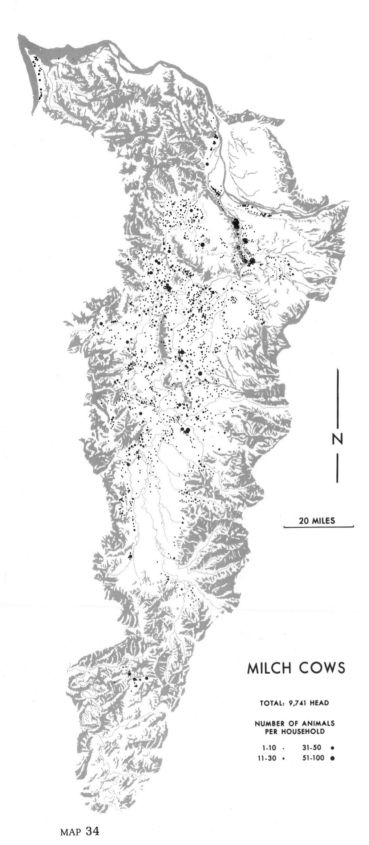

MILCH COWS

TOTAL: 9,741 HEAD

NUMBER OF ANIMALS
PER HOUSEHOLD

| 1-10 | . | 31-50 | ● |
| 11-30 | . | 51-100 | ● |

20 MILES

N

MAP 34

Richardson, emphasized dairying more than their neighbors, yet not even their cows' performance was particularly outstanding. Ownsbee's thirty-five cows produced only fifteen hundred pounds of butter and six hundred pounds of cheese, while Richardson's thirty-one animals made nine hundred pounds of butter and twenty-five hundred pounds of cheese. Elsewhere low production figures were even more striking. Daniel Waldo, owning about one hundred milk cows, reported no production as did G. W. Riches of Tualatin Plains who had sixty head; at Salem, James Force's eighty cows were listed by the 1850 agricultural census as producing one hundred pounds of butter; William Earl's seventy-two head on the South Santiam yielded five hundred pounds.

It is difficult to believe that Oregon's four largest herds of milch cows could have accounted for a combined production of only six hundred pounds of butter. Unaccounted milk production, although an important food source to farm families, could not have caused such low figures. Undoubtedly the fact that several census marshals were involved in the enumeration affected the results, but a large oversight seems unlikely, especially since Daniel O'Neill, who enumerated all the west side counties and Linn County, was thorough and careful in most other aspects of his census. Part of the answer to low butter production is perhaps found in a passing remark made by William Strong that "there were people in the valley where I stopped that had one hundred cows without milk or butter. They lived in that most primitive style, raising calves all the while."[4] Waldo, Force, and Earl certainly resembled this type. All had a fair number of other cattle besides their milkers.

As might have been expected, milkers were kept by more households than were beef cattle—15 percent more. The average herd size was seven animals, but less than half of Oregon's rural families had more than four cows.

Since the main function of the milch cow was to provide for the daily needs of the household, its distribution reflected that of the population (map 34), except that the ratio of cows to people was much lower in the towns than in the rural districts. In Polk County, for example, the figure was 1.4 animals per person, whereas in Portland the ratio was 4.4 persons per cow, a 600 percent difference. Considering the contrasting demographic, economic, and social characteristics of the two locales, this is not unexpected. Young men laboring for wages in towns, without home or family, could not be expected to keep cows. That was normally the work of women and older children. What does seem odd at first glance is that the urban deficit had not generated a concentration of dairy herds in the nearby farming communities.

The apparent failure of urban markets to influence the location of butter and cheese production may be assigned at least partially to the exceptionally rapid growth of the major towns. Portland was only four years old in 1850, and most of its population had arrived since 1849. Given the economic and physical limitations of frontier life, farmers simply could not convert to dairying rapidly enough to meet new demands—especially during a gold rush which found many farmers away from their homes for at least part of each year.

Cows of better breed were needed, but these were scarce and too costly for most men to purchase. Furthermore, dairymen such as Nicholas Ownsbee who had settled prior to market growth were faced with the prospect of relinquishing an established farm with good cheap land for perhaps illusory profits if they were to attempt to serve the new market. The certainty of existing claims and the uncertainty of resettlement in the wooded north weighed heavily in favor of the status quo.

In addition to their meat and dairy products, cattle provided one of the primary sources of power on the Oregon frontier. Beginning in 1843, the overland migrations used oxen almost exclusively to pull their heavily laden wagons across the continent. Experience showed that these seemingly ponderous animals had many advantages over horses or mules. They were better grazers and less likely to stray from camp. Most importantly they had tremendous stamina and could endure hardships that killed other animals. In his published guide to travel on the Oregon Trail, Joel Palmer, an immigrant of 1845, wrote, "Ox teams are more extensively used than any others. Oxen stand the trip much better and are not so liable to be stolen by the Indians and are much less trouble. Cattle are generally allowed to go at large when not hitched to the wagons; while horses and mules must always be staked out at night. Oxen can procure food in many places where horses cannot and in much less time."[5] The result of this practice was to provide almost every farmer with two or more yoke of oxen with

which to carry on the work of cultivation. Like milch cows, oxen were widely dispersed throughout the settlements (map 35), a normal household having on an average two yoke.

In his recollections of early plowing, J. Henry Brown noted, "There was not a span of horses hitched in the country. The first set of harness I ever saw in Oregon was in 1849 and it was brought from California. Here we used oxen altogether."[6] Strictly speaking this was not true. On French Prairie and, to a lesser extent, on the Tualatin Plains oxen were not so important as elsewhere. Many of the more successful farmers, especially the French Canadians, did not own even a single head. The reason can be traced to the settlement history of the two areas which unlike the rest of the frontier predated the common usage of oxen by several years. In 1837, William Slacum reported about forty yoke of oxen were used by the Hudson's Bay Company at their Fort Vancouver farm. The main draft animal of the company, however, and the only one with which most of the retired trappers were familiar was the horse, which could be obtained cheaply from interior tribes. By the time oxen could be easily acquired, horse herds had already been built up, and farming methods had become well-established.

Map 36 indicates the concentration of larger horse herds among the Canadian settlers of French Prairie. What it does not adequately portray is that even in the smallest classification of herds, containing between one and ten animals, the Canadians enjoyed a numerical advantage over the Americans. Typically, pioneers from the Middle West owned only one, two, or three horses, used almost exclusively with saddle. In contrast, Canadians often kept between eight and ten head.

Good horses were never difficult to obtain. The Cayuse, the Nez Perce, and some of the other tribes of the Columbia Plateau were talented breeders who produced sturdy, well-formed animals. These were so numerous that prior to the Gold Rush their value was kept low, the usual price for a healthy animal being between ten and twenty dollars. The main bloodlines of the frontier horse were Indian with an admixture of American types. Little is known about the American stock except that there were supposedly a fair number of high quality animals imported. Robert R. Thompson, who crossed the Great Plains in 1846, noted of his companions that "a great many of the people who composed the train were from

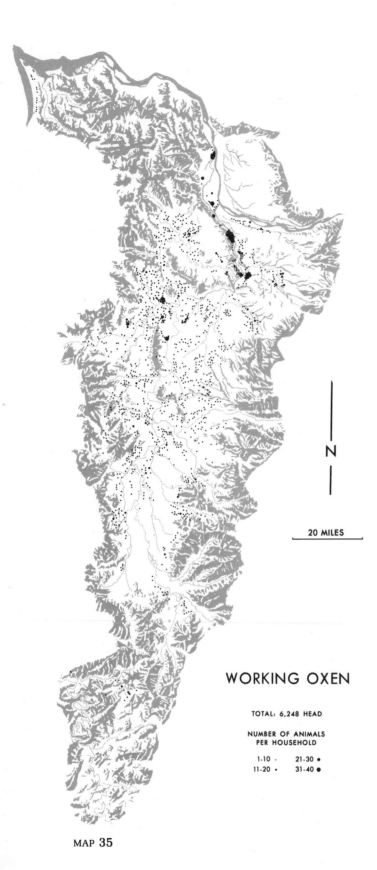

WORKING OXEN

TOTAL: 6,248 HEAD

NUMBER OF ANIMALS
PER HOUSEHOLD

1-10 ·	21-30 ●
11-20 •	31-40 ●

N

20 MILES

MAP 35

the then frontier states of Missouri, Illinois, Kentucky, and Tennessee, and also from Arkansas and a great many of them had fine horses—blooded stock. They came from districts where blooded horses were valued, where the people were passionately fond of good stock especially horses."[7]

Outside the older settlements large horse herds were connected at first almost exclusively with the more important cattle ranches. Hamilton Campbell, for instance, owned over one hundred animals. In 1848, however, increased demands fostered by the gold rush drove prices up to as much as one hundred dollars per head for Indian ponies. Interest in the commercial possibilities of raising horses increased, and some farmers began to pay more attention to their animals. By 1850 there were twelve herds with more than thirty head in Oregon.

Among stockmen there was apparently little interest in raising asses and mules. On the whole frontier only 309 were counted in 1850. Considering the southern origins of most of the rural population, this is difficult to understand. Missouri, Kentucky, and Tennessee were states where mules played an important economic role, and it is known that the animals were brought overland during the 1840s. One possibility is that the exorbitant prices paid for mules in California drained off the local supply in 1848 and 1849. Daniel Waldo had five mules that he sold in the California mines for three hundred dollars. Only 127 households had asses and mules, and of these 81 percent had fewer than three animals. If a team is defined as consisting of at least four animals, there were only sixteen mule teams in Oregon in 1850, and most of these belonged to pack trains!

More important than the mule, but numerically the least significant herd animal was the sheep. Its early history is not so well known as that of cattle. In 1837, Slacum reported that the Hudson's Bay Company owned about two hundred sheep. As with cattle, the first major importation was from California and was undertaken by the British firm. George B. Roberts, one of the Company's clerks, remembered the circumstances:

Mr. Douglas [afterwards Sir James] went to California in '40 with a permit obtained from Mexico to select 4,000 sheep. The Southern party of [the] company's trappers were to meet Douglas and joined then drove all through to the Tualatin plains—I sent in summer '41 to receive them distribute some, and crossed the rest over the Columbia—we simply swam them over in bands from Sauvie Island to the fishery on the north side and were doing this when Wilks' officers were surveying the Columbia River.[8]

There is some question as to who received sheep from Roberts. Map 37 indicates that in 1850 no Canadian family on French Prairie had a flock. In fact, the whole of northern Marion County had none. John Minto remembered Joseph Gervais running sheep in the bottoms near Salem in 1844, but six years later even these appear to have been given up. No reason for the complete absence of the animals in the district is discernible except for the possibility that both McLoughlin and the Canadians themselves saw no reason to keep them. Sheep needed almost constant attention and special knowledge for their proper management. Also, the technology of producing homespun from raw wool was a complex one requiring tools and training most of the trappers' native wives did not possess. These two factors may have been enough to keep sheep out of the district.

The animals Roberts distributed may have been given to the American missionaries. Alvin Smith mentioned that he had sheep, and it may be noted that in 1850 a number of former members of the Methodist Mission, such as Hamilton Campbell and Louis Judson, also had them. All this is conjecture, however, for by 1843 Joseph Gale and Jacob Lesse had brought a second band up from California, and it is probable that these were the foundation of the first American flocks.

California sheep were universally recognized among the pioneers as inferior animals. North of the Columbia, the Puget Sound Agriculture Company imported Southdowns to improve their stock, but none of these found their way south of the river. The exact year of importation of better sheep to the Willamette Valley is not known. It may be reasonably assumed that at least a few head were included in the 1843 immigration, for in 1844 Samuel Gilmore had a small band on the Yamhill River.

Small flocks seldom attracted attention. Consequently, little is known about most of the sheepherders with two notable exceptions, A. C. R. Shaw of Polk County and Joseph Watt, who settled near the confluence of Salt Creek with the Yamhill River. Both pioneers first came with Cornelius Gilliam's train in 1844, and both were influential in the introduction of American sheep to Oregon. In recalling the journey, Joseph Watt noted,

There were 16 sheep brought out by a man of the name of Shaw. . . . He started with them intending to kill

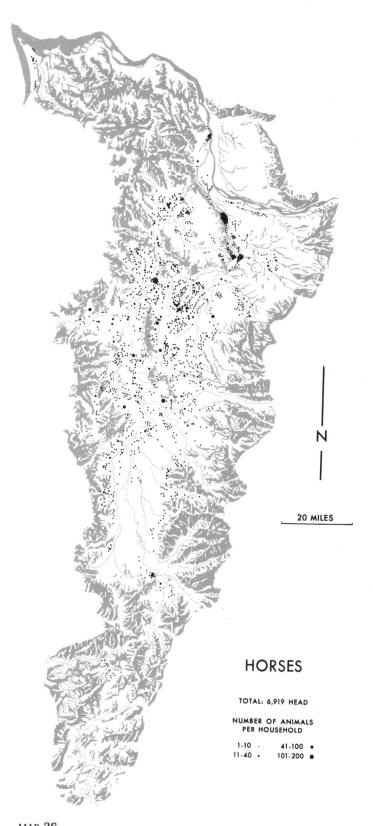

HORSES

TOTAL: 6,919 HEAD

NUMBER OF ANIMALS
PER HOUSEHOLD

1-10　·　　　41-100　●
11-40　·　　101-200　●

MAP 36

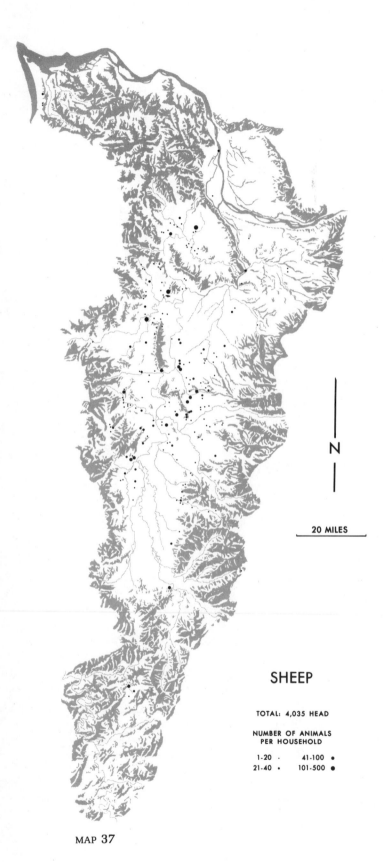

SHEEP

TOTAL: 4,035 HEAD

NUMBER OF ANIMALS
PER HOUSEHOLD

1-20 ·	41-100 •
21-40 •	101-500 ●

MAP 37

them for mutton, but he found he could not sell them, and that they could travel as fast as cattle. When we got out here we could not get any sheep. They were Spanish sheep brought here by the Hudson's Bay Company but they could not sell them. There was no cloth for the women; so I brought out a carding machine in 1847 and I brought some sheep with me at the same time.[9]

In 1847, five hundred sheep passed over the Barlow Road before November.

Within three more years sheep totaled slightly more than 4,000 head. The four largest flocks were owned by John Watt and Matthew Patten, both on the Yamhill, Walter Pomeroy on the Tualatin Plains, and A. C. R. Shaw near the mouth of the Rickreall. Others were located widely, but un-evenly, throughout the settlements. The only area of general distribution extended southward from Howell's Prairie to the Santiam River in Marion County. There flocks were of moderate to small size, only three exceeding fifty animals and most having fewer than twenty head. Elsewhere small clusters of flocks grazed along the Calapooya and Luckiamute rivers, in northern Benton County, in the vicinity of Lafayette, and on the southern Tualatin Plains.

Less is probably known about the pig than any other animal on the Oregon frontier. Considering its history and importance to the early settlers, the published literature has remained strangely mute. Apparently, in the mythical West of horses and cattle there is little room for so lowly an animal. Anonymity notwithstanding, swine were among the very first animals brought to Astoria and later taken inland to Fort Vancouver. When William A. Slacum visited the latter post in 1837, he reported the hog population numbered about seven hundred head. By then they had already spread southward across the Columbia River to Sauvie Island and up valley to the Canadian and Methodist settlements.

Like the Spanish cattle, hogs were ideally suited to frontier life. They were hardy creatures that demanded little attention, and although they lacked the defensive capabilities of the longhorns, they often made up for this with sheer pugnacity. Hogs were excellent gang fighters, ready to rush to the assistance of a herd member in distress. Furthermore they produced such large litters that their numbers rapidly multiplied. Versatility was the hog's outstanding virtue. No other domestic animal exhibited such facility and prowess in foraging for the necessities of life. If there was nothing to eat above ground, it would root up food from beneath the soil or even from underwater. Swine hardly ever died from starvation.

In the Willamette Valley, two native plants, the Oregon oak (*Quercus garryana*) and the camas (*Camassia quamash*), became especially important items in the pig's diet. Early visitors sometimes deprecated the quality of these foods. In his 1839 "Memoir" on Oregon, Nathaniel Wyeth stated that "hogs live and multiply, but cannot be made fat on the range of the country; there are no nuts except the hazel nut; acorns are plenty, and also many roots on which they feed; but for stock, this part of the country is in every respect inferior to the Middle and Western states."[10]

More recent investigations indicate that perhaps Wyeth underestimated the value of the acorns. After studying stands of small trees in the mountains of northern California in 1944, botanist Carl B. Wolf noted that in normal crop years the Oregon oak produced about five hundred pounds of acorns per acre. Allowing for the larger tree crowns characteristic of the central Willamette Valley's extensive oak woodlands and oak openings this figure might be increased by 50 percent or more. When multiplied by the thousands of acres covered by the trees in the 1840s, the harvest must have totaled millions of pounds. The nutritional qualities of the acorn also seem to have been quite good. According to Wolf's informants, pigs preferred the acorns of the Oregon oak to all others, and when fed on them produced a good grade of pork.

The other important source of native food for hogs was camas, a member of the lily family which occupied seasonal marshes and other poorly drained ground in the Pacific Northwest, northern California, and western Montana. The edible portion of the plant consists of onion-like bulbs approximately one inch in diameter. When carefully treated, these yielded a floury substance relatively rich in carbohydrate.

The food supply offered by the oaks and camas was so great and so easily obtained that swine multiplied rapidly and escaped into the woods. By the late 1830s, numerous bands of wild hogs roamed the countryside. Since so little interest was shown at the time in the activities of these animals it is now difficult to accurately assess the effects they had on the land. There are some suggestions that they had a tremendous impact on the native economy. By eating large amounts of camas and acorns, pigs effectively reduced the Indians' main supplies of carbohydrate. Their consumption was so great in some areas that bands of Indians were driven to near starvation. On March 27, 1854, Indian Superintendent Joel Palmer wrote a letter concerning the situation facing the Calapooya who still lived along the Tualatin River: "The Wappato, Kammas and other nutritious roots once produced abundantly in the marshes and lowlands around their principal residences, and constituting their principal means of subsistence, have, since the increase of swine, gradually diminished in quantity and must soon entirely fail."[11]

The ubiquitous hog also affected the lives of the settlers in many subtle ways. Its intelligence and perserverance in attacking cultivated crops required farmers to be especially diligent in their construction of sturdy fences. Its wanderings made herd surveillance almost impossible and resulted in confusion of ownership, poaching, and some theft. One of the few instances of crime in the early settlement of the Willamette dealt with "a settler who had been detected stealing his neighbor's pigs by enticing them to his house, dropping them into his cellar where they were slaughtered and afterwards eaten."[12]

As far as agriculture was concerned hogs added measurably to the efficiency of farming processes. Skim milk and whey that would otherwise have been discarded was fed to swine. Tremendous quantities of grain, potatoes, and other crops left in the fields by crude harvesting methods could also be utilized by these capable gleaners. No labor had to be expended, no instructions given, by merely turning a herd loose in a field, waste was converted into a valuable and easily transported product—pork.

Another advantage of the hog was its size. The combined weight of twelve animals slaughtered by Alvin Smith in February 1850 was 2,954 pounds, an average of 246 pounds per head. Assuming this was a normal figure, and the remainder of Smith's diary suggests this was the case, the frontier pig was usually a modest-sized animal. Descriptions also indicate that many wild hogs were not particularly rotund, but rather lean and long legged. The advantage of this small compact body was that it was more readily slaughtered, preserved, and eaten than the much larger cattle. Smoked hams, bacon, and salted pork were highly regarded foods which kept well without refrigeration, and as a result, they became staples of home consumption and commerce.

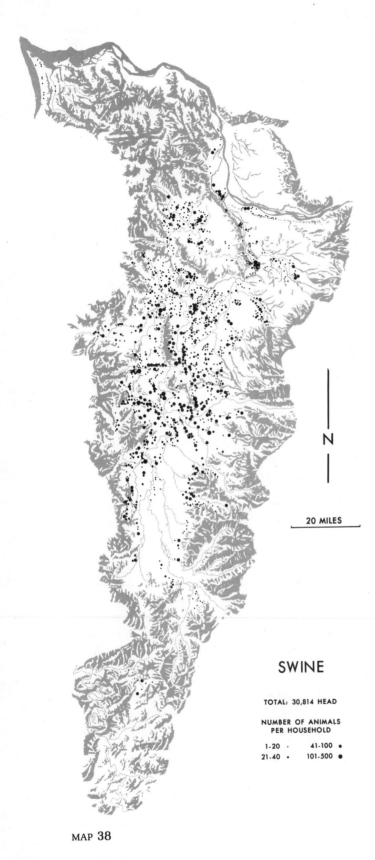

SWINE

TOTAL: 30,814 HEAD

NUMBER OF ANIMALS
PER HOUSEHOLD

1-20 ·	41-100 ●
21-40 ·	101-500 ●

20 MILES

N

MAP 38

Occasionally herds of swine were even driven south to the California mines.

By 1850 over thirty thousand swine were attached to pioneer households, and thousands more roamed unclaimed through the countryside. On an average this amounted to about twenty-five animals per farm. Herds containing up to fifty head were common, and as map 38 shows, they could be found almost everywhere except the Clatsop Plains, where their numbers were limited.

Within the general distribution, several areas of greater concentration and herd size may be identified. By far the most important of these extended southward from near the confluence of the Yamhill and Willamette rivers to the vicinity of the Luckiamute and Santiam rivers. Within this section herds commonly exceeded thirty or even fifty head, perhaps reflecting the greater availability of mast and camas in the woodlands and marshes of this portion of the valley.

The Oregon pioneer was not wholly dependent on livestock for his existence. Equally, if not more, important to the rural economy were plants. Wheat was the most important crop of the frontier. It fed the populace, supported local industry, and entered channels of foreign trade. As the chief export it paid for those few necessities and small luxuries so important for survival. The grain was first grown at Fort Vancouver, and from there it spread southward to the Canadian settlement and Jason Lee's mission. Little is known about its genetic character, except that at least two types were commonly cultivated by the mid 1840s. One was known as "spring red" and was bearded like rye. The Methodists raised this variety at their Mission farm in Marion County, and from there it was spread by American colonists throughout the valley. The other strain was an even more anonymous type usually called "white seed wheat."

Agricultural practices were primitive and often little care was given to efficient grain production. Philip Edwards noted that "the ground without manure produces from fifteen to twenty bushels of wheat per acre, varying with the culture and season, and I should not omit to observe that the cultivation is quite defective."[13] Likewise Lieutenant Neil M. Howison reported, "the average yield is twenty bushels to the acre; and this from very slovenly culture. Those who take much pains, reap forty or fifty."[14] Every step in the process was done in a most primitive manner. The plows were crude wooden devices; the seed was sown by hand. Harvesting was accomplished with the cradle, and in medium grain two men were able to cut and bind about three or four acres a day. Next, the grain had to be separated from the straw. Peter Crawford recalled that in 1848:

The thrashing was tardy and slow—a floor was made in the field by fencing in a circular patch with rails in the wheat field turn in a lot of Cayouses or even oxen and cows and steers Drive around and around until the ground was firm then haul in a lot of wheat in the sheaf or bundle Put them in very thick—not loosing the sheaves, turn in the cayouses tame and wild drive around and around until well thrashed haul out the shock and thrash and stack Some of the grain near the correll.[15]

According to Lincoln Wilkes three such floorings a day was the usual rate.

In 1848, the mechanical thresher made its first appearance south of the Columbia. Messrs. Wallace and Wilson of Oregon City built two threshing machines which did a good business in the Tualatin Plains and elsewhere in the Willamette Valley during the summer and fall. As described by John E. Ross, who was hired in August 1848 to run one of the new devices, they were driven by an "endless chain which was powered by four mules." During the gold rush, however, both machines seem to have disappeared, and the farmers reverted to their earlier methods.

Few figures exist to document annual wheat production during the 1840s. One of the seemingly more reliable estimates appeared in the January 7, 1847 edition of the Oregon City *Spectator*. According to the paper, the 1846 wheat harvest totaled approximately 150,000 bushels. About 60,000 bushels were produced in Champoeg (Marion) County, 30,000 bushels in Tualatin (Washington) County, 20,000 bushels in Yamhill, 15,000 bushels in Polk, and probably less than 20,000 bushels in Clatsop and Clackamas counties. The accuracy of at least the Yamhill production was substantiated by county assessor W. T. Newby, who reported the harvest at 24,546 bushels. By dividing the total production by an average yield of twenty bushels to the acre, we arrive at an estimated area of about 7,500 acres planted in wheat.

Comparison of the yields of the 1846 crop and the 208,305 bushels enumerated in the 1850 census indicates that in the intervening years production increased only by one third, a rather low figure considering the reputation for rapid growth enjoyed by the Oregon frontier. Even more

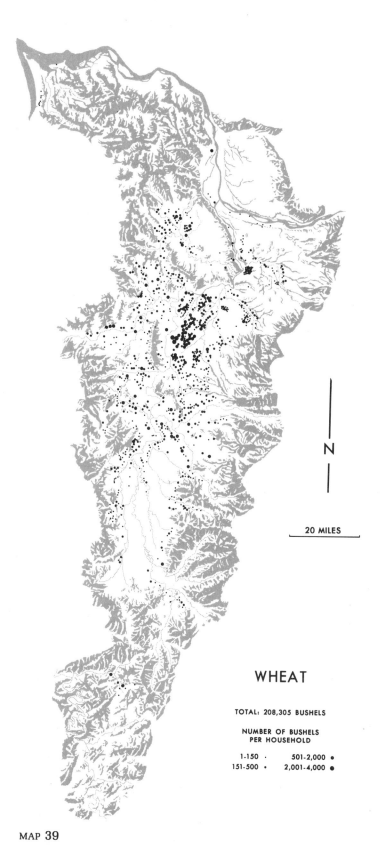

WHEAT

TOTAL: 208,305 BUSHELS

NUMBER OF BUSHELS
PER HOUSEHOLD

1-150 ·   501-2,000 •
151-500 •   2,001-4,000 ●

MAP 39

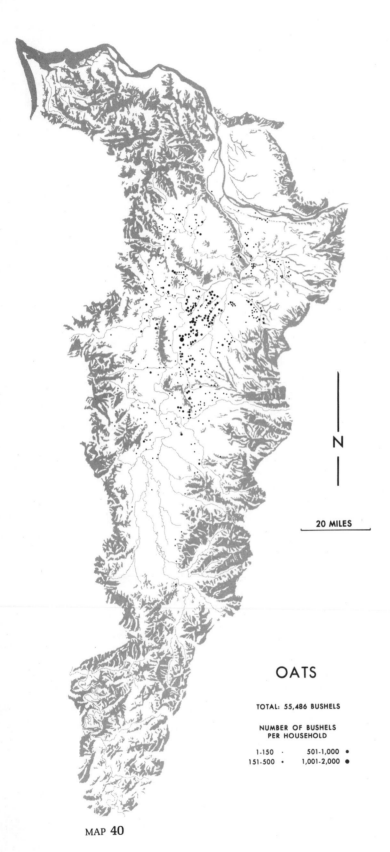

N

20 MILES

OATS

TOTAL: 55,486 BUSHELS

NUMBER OF BUSHELS
PER HOUSEHOLD

| 1-150 | · | 501-1,000 | ● |
| 151-500 | · | 1,001-2,000 | ● |

MAP 40

surprising are the data that show either no significant advance or a decrease in Clackamas, Washington, Yamhill, and Polk counties. There is always the chance that serious errors were included in crop estimates, but confirmation of the 1846 Yamhill harvest by two sources at least suggests that this did not occur in the first set of figures.

Checking the accuracy of the 1850 census is a more complex problem, for it is possible that the four United States census marshals did not follow published instructions, but instead computed crop yields in different and perhaps incompatible ways. Although many farms had no production listed at all, analysis of the manuscript census schedules does not show any identifiable sampling bias. All sizes of wheat yields were noted from the smallest to the largest, and no areas were ignored. It does indicate, however, a remarkable concentration of larger than average production units on French Prairie (map 39). Fifteen of Oregon's nineteen farms raising more than one thousand bushels of wheat were located in this single district. Together these fifteen produced about 14 percent of the frontier's entire crop.

The census forms themselves suggest one possible reason for the general absence of wheat and other field crops on many farms. This is that the wording of the schedules stipulated that the yields to be counted were those of the year *ending* June 1850, in other words, the summer harvest of 1849. Since the Oregon census was exceedingly drawn out it seems reasonable that farmers might have responded with figures dealing with their most recent harvest, that of July and August 1850. If the census marshals followed their instructions to the letter, however, they would have specifically requested data for the prior year, diminishing totals to those of a gold rush year.

Although it cannot be proven that confusion in interpreting administrative instructions led to the collection of incompatible data from two different harvests, the small wheat yields and general absence of cultivation on many farms indicate that the effect of the California gold rush on the agricultural economy of Oregon may not have been entirely beneficial. Using an average yield of twenty bushels per acre, an approximation of wheat field acreage is obtained showing that usually the ground planted in wheat amounted to no more than two and one-half to twenty-five acres. Such low figures probably reflect the neglect associated with the feverish excitement that swept through the Oregon settlements after the discovery of gold. In the spring and summer of 1848 and 1849, men left families and farms in search of fortune. Existing fields were hurriedly planted and then abandoned to the care of the women and children. Improvements and maintenance were postponed, crops were not adequately cared for, and as a result, agriculture generally stagnated for two years.

Oats, the second most important cereal grown in Oregon, accounted for only 55,486 bushels, and since much of this was fed to animals, its cultivation was usually restricted to the more substantial and profitable farms, where the owners' food requirements had already been satisfied. As map 40 indicates, few of the more recently established farms on the fringes of settlement raised oats. The crop was especially concentrated on French Prairie. There a large proportion of the farmers planted the grain, and average holdings yielded harvests of 150 to 250 bushels. Elsewhere most growers harvested fewer than fifty bushels a year.

French Prairie farmers were also the most important cultivators of beans and peas. Together, legumes yielded a harvest of 3,566 bushels, hardly a major contribution to the economy of the frontier. The significance of these crops lies not in their monetary value, but in their high correlation with French Canadian population (map 41). Most farms on the prairie north of Salem had at least a small acreage in peas and beans, whereas in the rest of the valley they were virtually ignored.

The one important field crop not prominent in commercial trade was the Irish potato. With a caloric value less than one quarter that of wheat and its greater susceptibility to spoilage, it could not bear the high cost of transport. Its main advantage, like that of the pig, was its success in a wide range of primitive environments without constant attention. From the establishment of Astoria onward, potatoes were grown wherever there were settlers. They became a medium of exchange for farmers who hired starving immigrants to build fences, and many families survived almost entirely on the tubers for the first year or more.

The common dependence of the newcomers on this staple was recalled by Peter Burnett:

For the first two years after our arrival in Oregon we were frequently without any meat for weeks at a time. On these occasions if we had milk, butter, and potatoes we were well content. In May 1845, we were entirely without anything in the house for dinner. I did not

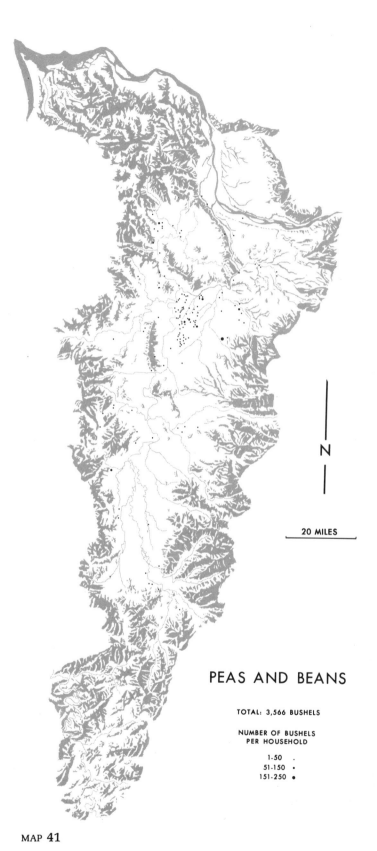

PEAS AND BEANS

TOTAL: 3,566 BUSHELS

NUMBER OF BUSHELS
PER HOUSEHOLD

1-50   .
51-150   ·
151-250 ●

MAP 41

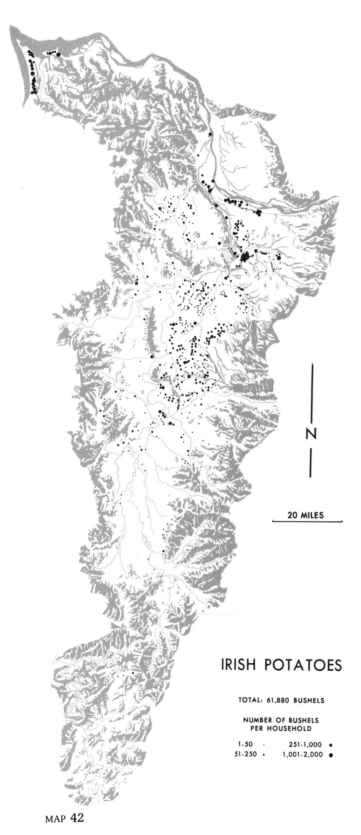

IRISH POTATOES

TOTAL: 61,880 BUSHELS

NUMBER OF BUSHELS
PER HOUSEHOLD

1-50   ·   251-1,000   •
51-250   ·   1,001-2,000   ●

20 MILES

N

MAP 42

know what to do, when my wife suggested a remedy. The year before we had cultivated a small patch of potatoes, and in digging had left some in the ground, which had sprung up among the young wheat. We dug up a mess of these potatoes, which sufficed us for a meal, though not very good.[16]

Since potatoes could not be profitably shipped any great distance, farmers seldom grew more than could be used at home or in the neighborhood. Throughout most of the upper Willamette Valley production was dispersed and typically smaller than fifty bushels. Only in the more heavily forested and urbanized north did farmers make a specialty of commercial root cultivation (map 42). Phillip Foster, whose farm on the Clackamas River was one of the first met after crossing over the Cascades from The Dalles on Barlow's Road, raised two thousand bushels of potatoes for the immigrant trade. John Switzler, operator of the ferry across the Columbia River to Fort Vancouver, produced one thousand bushels, and Henderson Luelling, pioneer nurseryman living on the outskirts of Milwaukie, grew another one thousand bushels. Potato farmers were also located on the overflow lands of Sauvie Island and along the south side of the Columbia River.

On the Clatsop Plains the effect of proximity to a small urban market and commercial shipping was reinforced by a climate and soil ill-suited for the cultivation of wheat. Salmon and potatoes were dietary staples. The latter were initially obtained from trader James Birnie's garden at old Fort George, and were probably direct descendents of the first potatoes brought to the Northwest by Astor's men. By 1850, twenty farmers were producing 8,280 bushels of the crop, an average of more than four hundred bushels per grower.

Farmers on the Clatsop Plains also excelled in market gardening. Ships' crews provided a lucrative market for fresh vegetables, and the low-lying, organic soils and cool maritime climate combined to produce good harvests. In 1850 almost $28,000 worth of vegetables was raised by two dozen farmers. This was very different from the Willamette Valley, where vegetable production was mostly limited to household needs and valued at one hundred dollars or less per farm. The only inland area of large commercial gardens was located in the vicinity of the northern towns and along the Columbia River (map 43).

Although the family garden did not usually account for much income, its importance should not be underestimated, for only homegrown vegetables allowed the pioneers to escape the tedium of a normally dull and unbalanced diet. Sometimes garden produce was the only thing keeping a household from hunger. Even mighty Joe Meek was on at least one occasion forced to subsist on his squashes.

Almost every conceivable type of vegetable was grown. Lincoln Wilkes remembered cabbage, beans, peas, pumpkins, turnips, tomatoes, carrots, parsnips, onions, and rutabagas. Peter Burnett added lettuce and squashes to the list, and there were also several different types of melons. All were eaten fresh or, as in the case of string beans and onions, air dried and stored for winter.

By 1850 many of the more improved farms also had young orchards, but except for the older plantings of the French Canadians, few trees had matured sufficiently to bear more than a token harvest. In all the frontier, only eight individuals were credited with any noteworthy production, and of this number just two, Etienne Lucier and Achilles Peault, were important orchardists. Both men had obtained seeds from Fort Vancouver at an early date. When Ralph Geer first saw the French Prairie orchards in 1847, he judged that the trees might have already been planted twenty years. The three most common were the apple, pear, and peach, and all had been grown from seeds.

Grafted fruit trees were unknown until 1847, when William Meek and Henderson Luelling brought a nursery of seven hundred trees overland. Others attempted the same feat. In the year of Meek's and Luelling's crossing, Joel Palmer lost a nursery on the Deschutes River and was able to salvage only a small number of seeds. The man in charge of Palmer's venture was Ralph C. Geer, who later remembered, "I brought two bushels of apple and pear seeds. I gave half of them to my father, and they were put out on the Clackamas River. From my pear seeds sprung all the pear orchards in this country. I sold the seedlings to Luelling and William Meek."[17]

The land was new, and during the early years of experimental planting, opinions varied as to the proper methods of cultivation. At first the farmers who were used to harsh eastern winters thought that fruit trees could not be raised from seeds without colder temperatures. Also, it was widely believed that because of the tremendous numbers of rodents in Oregon, seeds had to be

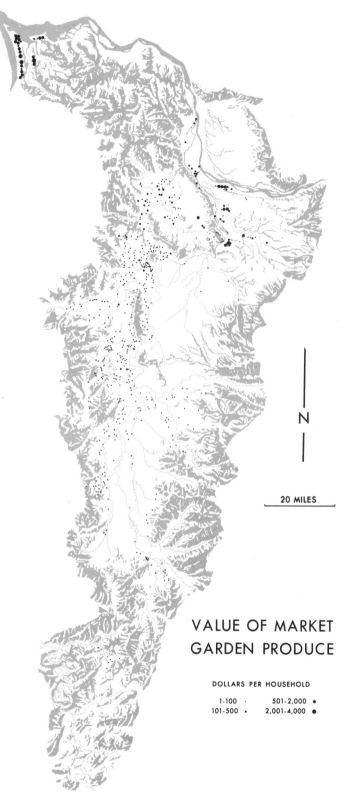

N

20 MILES

VALUE OF MARKET
GARDEN PRODUCE

DOLLARS PER HOUSEHOLD

| 1-100 | · | 501-2,000 | • |
| 101-500 | · | 2,001-4,000 | ● |

MAP 43

planted on islands to survive. As a consequence, the establishment of orchards was somewhat retarded.

Fruit trees, gardens, cattle, and grain—each type of crop and livestock contributed in some degree to the creation of Oregon's agricultural base. In the unspecialized rural economy of the frontier, single products hardly ever provided the sole support of a farm. Diversification was the watchword, diversification to match the farmer's capabilities with family needs, commercial demands, and the restrictions of the physical environment. As these factors changed, so also did the combination of crops upon which the rural economy was founded. By 1850, interaction between man and the land had already led to the development of several subtly defined agricultural districts, each with a character slightly different from the next. In all, some form of general farming based upon both livestock and cultivation dominated the economy, but in every one the processes of selection were creating a separate identity.

The most distinctive of the regionalized economies was that of the Clatsop Plains. There, immediate access to Astoria and its shipping combined with the physical restrictions of the littoral environment to accentuate the production of perishable commodities. Fresh vegetables, potatoes, and dairy products were the mainstays of farms strung out along the strand behind the last line of dunes. Additional income was derived from fishing and the collection of wild cranberries.

Upstream from Milton City along the low-lying margins of the Columbia and in the immediate vicinity of the larger towns, perishables also dominated agricultural production. There farmers expended most of their labor cultivating potatoes and vegetables and tending to their milch cows. On Sauvie Island there was an especially close resemblance to farming on the coast.

In the Willamette Valley above Oregon City root crops and market gardens were commercially less significant. Greater emphasis was placed on the cultivation of grain and raising livestock. Comparison of the relative importance of these two activities indicates the mixed farming economy of the inland settlements varied from one district to the next, the most striking example being on the prairies of Marion County between Champoeg and Salem, where French Canadians and others paid greater attention to the cultivation of wheat and oats than in any other part of the frontier. French Prairie was the center of commercial grain production. From this one area came most of the wheat exported to the Northwest Coast and California. Beef cattle and swine were merely secondary concerns, and dairying was restricted almost entirely to the satisfaction of household needs.

South and east of the Pudding River, from the Mollala settlements to the forks of the Santiam, stretched a second agricultural district in which the various aspects of mixed farming were more nearly balanced. Although harvests were smaller, sufficient grain was grown for export. Potatoes were raised in commercial quantities, as were cattle and pigs in the south. In part, the unspecialized character of the farms was due to their age. Few had been established more than several years, and the amount of improved land averaged less than forty acres per claim. Where settlement was of longer standing, such as on Howell Prairie and in the vicinity of the old Methodist Mission near Salem, improved acreages were greater as was the relative importance of grain production.

The Tualatin Valley was another area in which the cultivated crops and livestock shared almost equally in the support of a rural community. Proximity to the urban markets of Portland, Oregon City, and Linn City tended to direct slightly more attention toward market gardens and other perishables, but overall, little preference was shown for any particular item.

South of Washington County the balance of agricultural activity shifted increasingly in favor of livestock. The amount of improved acreage attached to farms decreased as did the cash value of properties. Concurrently, herd size and frequency increased. On the Yamhill wheat shared its importance with beef cattle and dairy products. Between the Rickreall and Marys rivers swine assumed a dominant position, and from the Luckiamute southward to the Belknap Settlement, dairy products contributed relatively more to the rural economy than elsewhere in the valley.

Conclusion

HERE WE CLOSE our discussion of the Oregon frontier—not because the subject has been thoroughly explored, but because a beginning has been made. A society, even a small one, is a complex world that defies simple description and analysis. The diversity of physical landscape and human experience is so great that in attempting a comprehensive work one may be tempted to resort to gross oversimplification or bury the reader under an avalanche of detail.

To avoid some of the hazards of such a study of life on the edge of wilderness, this investigation has limited itself to a few of the salient topics related to the developing frontier landscape of early Oregon. It is hoped that the selection has been adequate to illustrate the basic geography of pioneer life in one part of the Pacific Northwest and, at least partially, to answer the primary questions of who, what, where, and why. At the same time, it is hoped that the almost total exclusion of many vital subjects will itself motivate the reader to further inquiry. An invitation is particularly extended to those who, like the author, believe that the systematic mapping of past landscapes is an essential prerequisite to perceptive historical analysis.

Many of the topics included in the text, and others not even considered, deserve closer scrutiny. Motivation, for instance, is an essential factor governing human behavior. Yet, little of consequence concerning the impetus behind the overland migrations has appeared to test the simplistic explanations offered by economic determinists or the patriotic declarations of political romanticists. The weight of Oregon's pioneer literature argues convincingly that a search for good health brought many, if not most, settlers west. The greater question of the place of disease in the history and geography of the entire West, however, remains to be answered.

Likewise, the process of acquiring information in the technologically primitive, semiliterate society of nineteenth-century America is worthy of additional investigation. The role of the clan in the overland migration and settlement of Oregon was indeed important—particularly in the rural districts. But, it is uncertain how much longer this phenomenon of highly selective personal communication influenced the frontier or how significant it was elsewhere.

Among the clan's most noteworthy effects was its tendency to perpetuate existing sectional divisions between comunities. Oregon's frontier population was not a homogeneous one. To a remarkable degree it was quite the opposite. Nowhere is this more apparent than in the striking contrasts that existed between the rural and urban populations. The agricultural districts drew a disproportionate share of their people from the Middle West and Upper South while the towns attracted more unmarried men from Europe and the northeastern states. By 1850, two geographically and demographically distinct frontier populations had established themselves, a condition which is partially reflected by the fact that all the Willamette Valley counties not bearing Indian names were dedicated to southern heroes, whereas town names with eastern antecedents, such as Salem and Portland, were northern in character.

One result of the large southern element in the rural districts was that the political allegiance of the Willamette Valley's electorate was firmly attached to the Democratic party. Prior to the Civil War, Whigs and Republicans made respectable showings only in the northern towns and later in the mines of southern Oregon. Division of public sentiment over the slavery question, passage of anti-Negro legislation, growth of Know-Nothing philosophy, and perhaps even the much later ascendancy of the Klu Klux Klan may be traced to the cultural heritage of the first farmers.

The ultimate effects of this dichotomy on the social history of Oregon has still to be determined. It left its mark on all aspects of frontier life. Occupations reflected place of birth to a considerable degree, the rural trades being largely dominated by men from the Middle West, while those related to commerce and industry were usually the preserve of easterners and Europeans. Religious denominations also underlined ethnic differences. Methodist, Baptist, and Campbellite congregations were common everywhere, except French Prairie. Presbyterian and Congregational churches, on the other hand, were generally located in the towns.

Motivation, and the processes of information diffusion, were important determinants in the frontier experience, but they did not operate alone. The physical landscape, particularly the vegetation and the condition of the rivers, affected the location of settlement. Farmers were attracted to the Willamette Valley's prairie margins where the proximity of open ground and forest provided a diversity of necessary natural resources not found elsewhere. Millers, merchants, and associated tradesmen settled mainly at sites where there was waterpower for industrialization or navigable water for commerce.

The problems faced by the immigrants and the solutions they devised for conquering the wilderness reflect the pioneer's perception of the land and his relationship to it. Moralistic pronouncements of modern idealists notwithstanding, the Oregon frontiersmen found little to admire in either splendid isolation or communal living. Out of necessity they bound themselves to their neighbors and to the greater society, but the basic motivating force was economic survival not social philanthropy, a fact which is apparent in the daily records of the pioneers. Goods and services might have been loaned to the needy to ensure their survival, but they were hardly ever given without expectation of repayment. Even the most impoverished immigrants were expected to exchange their labor for the necessities of life. From 1843 until the California gold rush, it was the market created by these hungry survivors of each year's migration that provided the driving force for agricultural improvement and general economic growth. The typical Oregon farm was a commercial enterprise, not merely a subsistence operation.

A review of the preceding chapters suggests additional comments concerning the historical geography of early Oregon and the quality of life on the frontier, but since the bulk of the investigation has been devoted to the preliminary step of cartographic description it seems presumptuous to prolong this summary or to speak yet of significant conclusions. Certainly, the maps themselves offer fresh insights into the complex relationships that exist between men and the land. They are truly original contributions to the historical geography of the West. Maps, however, are not just final statements. They are also new sources of information which may lead future researchers to yet unanticipated subjects and discoveries.

Today there exists a great untapped wealth of geographic information in federal, state, and local archives, information so complete that new, accurate maps of America's historical landscapes may be constructed. Oregon shows us that through hard work apparently unrelated records may be successfully combined to define more clearly the past condition of a land and the people who inhabited it.

APPENDIX I

Cartographic Resources and Mapping the 1850 Census

LANGUAGE occupies so central a place in our existence that we are often inclined to forget that information and ideas may be expressed in other forms. The use of the map in historical studies of the American West is a case in point. Although potentially one of the most efficient and sophisticated investigative tools, it has generally been an inconsequential addendum to the central theme of literary research, a picturesque diagram best suited for the decoration of a book's dust jacket.

One of this study's central objects has been to produce an original cartographic statement of a major American frontier—a descriptive atlas which would prove useful to researchers interested in western history in its broadest sense. To this end, every attempt has been made to create a series of small-scale maps that cannot be excelled in their completeness, detail, and accuracy. The data source chosen as the basis for the project was the manuscript schedules of the Seventh United States Census. Earlier censuses had been taken in Oregon in 1845 and 1849, but neither approached the detail of the 1850 count.

Between September 6, 1850, and March 9, 1851, federal census marshals compiled the single most complete demographic and economic record for early Oregon.[1] Comparisons with all other relevant materials indicate that, allowing for the *de jure* count and the fact that the enumeration continued for a period of six months, the corrected figure of 11,873 persons is probably within 5 percent of the actual number of inhabitants then residing in the settlements south of the Columbia River.

Altogether six schedules were included in the 1850 census. These were (1) free inhabitants, (2) slave inhabitants, (3) mortality, (4) agriculture, (5) industry, and (6) social statistics. Only the lists pertaining to free inhabitants, agriculture, and industry contained data appropriate for mapping.[2]

Schedule number 1, relating to free inhabitants, consisted of over 280 manuscript pages listing individuals living in Oregon south of the Columbia River according to county of residence. The format of the schedule provided thirteen columns for the registration of the number of dwellings and families visited; the name of every person and his age, sex, and color; the occupation of males over fifteen years of age; the value of real estate owned; place of birth; whether married or attending school within the year; whether unable to read or write; and whether deaf and dumb, blind, insane, idiotic, a pauper, or convict (figure 3).

The first column in schedule 1, the dwelling, was of particular interest, for it facilitated mapping by grouping individuals in their residences. Observe in figure 3 that census marshals normally registered household members according to their status, the owner almost always taking precedence. In the normal home this meant the husband, who was followed by his wife, his children in order of decreasing age, and finally by any other persons not included within the immediate family. The latter might have been relatives (brothers-in-law were common), but more often were employees or temporary guests. Besides the private home, the term dwelling included hotels and boarding houses in the larger towns, and even ships.

From a strictly geographic standpoint the dwelling number was an indicator of relative location. The usual procedure followed by Oregon's census marshals when canvassing a district was to enumerate households in order of visitation. Starting at the end of a road, each residence was listed in turn until all were included. Then the process was begun again along another path with perhaps a break to pick up a stray or forgotten house. The result was an ordering of households that traced the route of a marshal's journey with remarkable fidelity. If the exact locations of a moderate number of residences could be identified, the locations of the remainder might be interpolated with some accuracy. An example of this linear organization of places is shown in map 44.

Numerous uses were suggested by the all-inclusive and detailed nature of the information contained within schedule 1, but because of the peculiar geographic order of the names and the microfilm format, rapid recall and use of specific data were impossible. Convenience determined that some mechanical means of data manipulation had to be employed if the census was to be used effectively as a research tool. Therefore, the state, county, census date, dwelling number, name, age, sex, birthplace, and occupation of each individual were coded, keypunched, and transferred to magnetic tape for computer processing.

Use of digital computers permitted the systematic generation of a variety of demographic computations and special lists. The most important of these was an alphabetic directory of the entire frontier population.

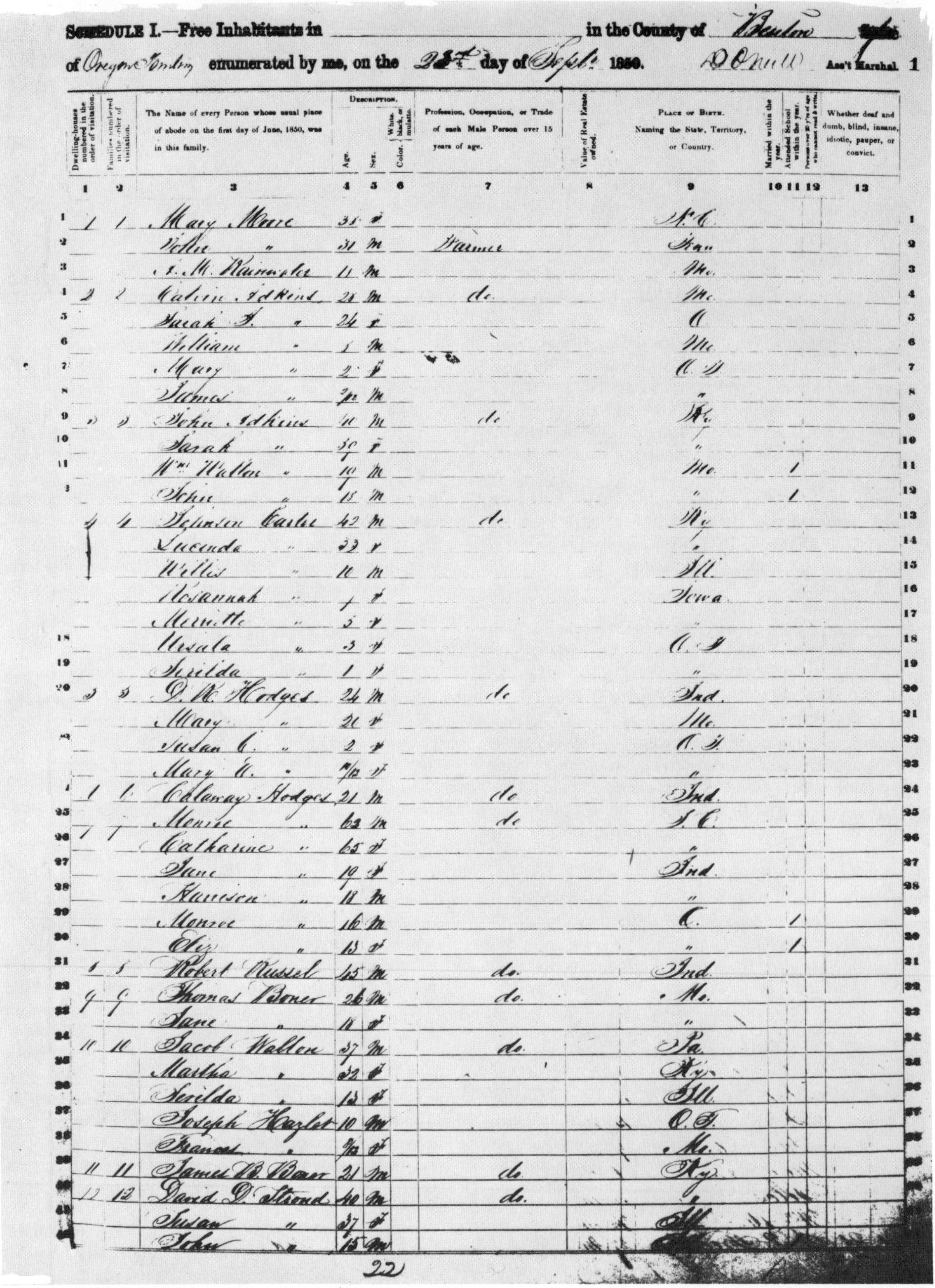

FIGURE 3. 1850 Population Census Schedule

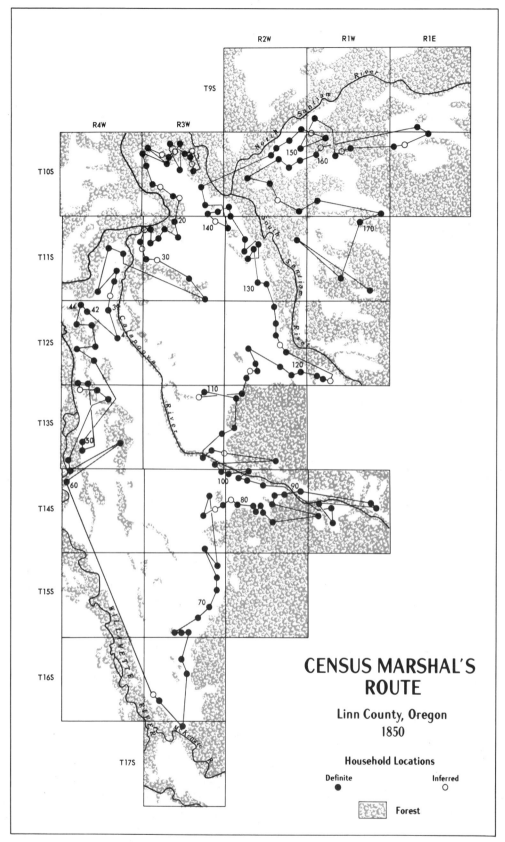

CENSUS MARSHAL'S ROUTE

Linn County, Oregon
1850

Household Locations

Definite   Inferred
●   ○

▨ Forest

MAP **44**

With this list erroneous double entries were eliminated, and, more importantly, all literary sources were opened for the first time to systematic analysis. Card files of libraries and archives that otherwise defied thorough investigation yielded immense numbers of references, which were combed for biographical and historical information. The thousands of bits of material that resulted were assembled into a simple data bank.

Financial and time restrictions limited computerization to the first schedule of the 1850 census. Because of their small size, utilization of the schedules of mortality, industry, and social statistics was not materially affected, but full use of the exceedingly long and complex section on the rural economy was seriously impaired.

The agricultural schedule consisted of forty-five double pages of tabular entries and included within it data pertaining to approximately 1,730 households. Forty or forty-one farms were listed on a full page, and the information concerning each was arranged in forty-six vertical columns (figures 4 and 5). About half of these were normally used by the census marshals.

In the first column, each farm was identified by the name of its owner or manager. The property itself was itemized under four broad categories: land, equipment, livestock, and crops. Land was the first considered and was classified as either improved or unimproved, often only the improved acreage being listed. Improved was a qualitative term which in Oregon apparently included ground that had been fenced and at least partially cultivated. One exception to this definition existed in the Clackamas County records where the speculative enthusiasm of the citizenry combined with the exaggerated assessments of the inimitable Joe Meek measurably inflated estimates of improvements and their worth.

Most categories included in the agricultural census required only simple enumeration of fairly well-defined quantities. In these, little discrepancy attributable to personal bias is found. Several classifications, however, such as the amount of improved acreage or cash value of a farm, demanded a more subjective estimate. As a result, significant error was introduced into the data. In the case of improved acreage, three marshals apparently decided that the definition should include only land enclosed within a fence. Limited agricultural production and large acreage figures for Clackamas County properties indicate, on the other hand, that Joseph Meek employed another measure, perhaps the claimants' responses. Consequently, data for this county cannot be compared with those of any other.

The effect of personal judgment is even more strikingly exemplified in the matter of property evaluation, where cash values were based upon not only the value of the cleared land, the quality of the soil, improvements such as buildings and fences, and the location of the property in respect to markets, but also the personal prejudices of farmer and enumerator. Every census marshal seems to have had a different scale. Joseph Meek's was an expansive one, that when combined with the speculative ambitions of town boomers and petty land agents, drove prices up to impossible heights. Lot Whitcomb thought that his unsold portion of Mil-

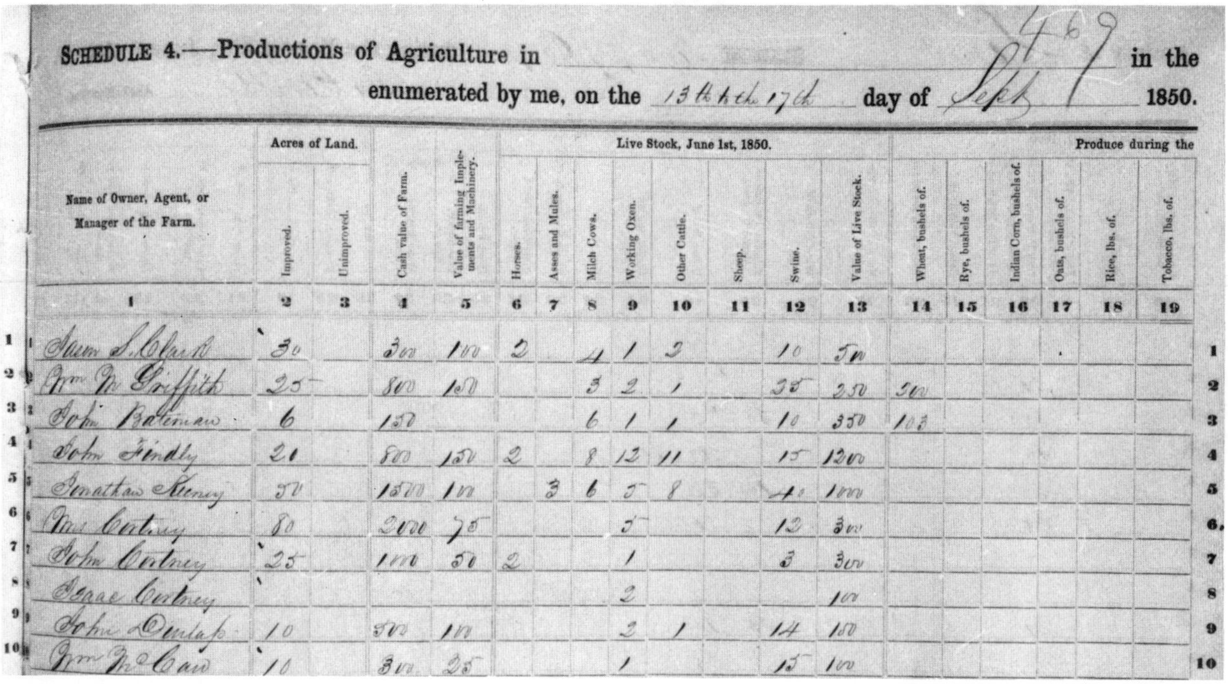
SCHEDULE 4.—Productions of Agriculture in ______ in the ______ enumerated by me, on the 13th 14th 17th day of Sept 1850.

	Name of Owner, Agent, or Manager of the Farm.	Acres of Land. Improved.	Unimproved.	Cash value of Farm.	Value of farming Implements and Machinery.	Live Stock, June 1st, 1850. Horses.	Asses and Mules.	Milch Cows.	Working Oxen.	Other Cattle.	Sheep.	Swine.	Value of Live Stock.	Produce during the ... Wheat, bushels of.	Rye, bushels of.	Indian Corn, bushels of.	Oats, bushels of.	Rice, lbs. of.	Tobacco, lbs. of.	
	1	2	3	4	5	6	7	8	9	10	11	12	13	14	15	16	17	18	19	
1	Sam S. Clark	30		300	100	2		4	1	2		10	500							1
2	Wm W. Griffith	25		800	150			3	2	1		35	250	500						2
3	John Bateman	6		150				6	1	1		10	350	103						3
4	John Findly	21		800	150	2		8	12	11		15	1200							4
5	Jonathan Keeney	50		1500	100		3	6	5	8		40	1000							5
6	Wm Cortney	80		2000	75				5			12	300							6
7	John Cortney	25		1000	50	2			1			3	300							7
8	Isaac Cortney								2				100							8
9	John Dunlap	10		500	100				2	1		14	150							9
10	Wm McCaw	10		300	25				1			15	100							10

FIGURE 4. 1850 Agriculture Census Schedule

County of _Linn_   State of _Territory of Oregon_ during the Year ending June 1, 1850, as _____ _D. O'Neill_ Ass't Marshal.

Year ending June 1, 1850.

Ginned Cotton, bales of 400 lbs. each.	Wool, lbs. of.	Peas & Beans, bush. of.	Irish Potatoes, bush. of.	Sweet Potatoes, bush. of.	Barley, bushels of.	Buckwheat, bushels of.	Value of Orchard Products in dollars.	Wine, gallons of.	Value of Produce of Market Gardens.	Butter, lbs. of.	Cheese, lbs. of.	Hay, tons of.	Clover Seed, bush. of.	Other Grass Seeds, bushels of.	Hops, lbs. of.	Hemp. Dew Rotted, tons of.	Hemp. Water Rotted, tons of.	Flax, lbs. of.	Flaxseed, bushels of.	Silk Cocoons, lbs. of.	Maple Sugar, lbs. of.	Cane Sugar, hhds. of 1,000 lbs.	Molasses, gallons of.	Beeswax and Honey, lbs. of.	Value of Home-made Manufactures	Value of Animals slaughtered.
20	21	22	23	24	25	26	27	28	29	30	31	32	33	34	35	36	37	38	39	40	41	42	43	44	45	46
									75																	
		20							75																	
		20						50	75																	
		10							300	50																50
		20							10	30																20
		20							20																	4
		20						50	150																	
									75																	

FIGURE 5. 1850 Agriculture Census Schedule (second page)

waukie was worth $200,000 and "farms" without cultivated crops were valued between $3,000 and $20,000. Clatsop County properties were likewise given exaggerated values, but at least here there was usually some improvement worth assessment. Improvements, not speculation, apparently influenced W. H. Rees's figures, so reliable comparisons can be made between Marion County farms. Daniel O'Neill also used improvements as the major determinant, and of all the enumerators, his estimates probably best reflect the true value of the land.

Recognizing the very real discrepancies that existed between the evaluations of adjacent counties in this single census, we might well question the validity of employing such data as indicators of socioeconomic status. In recent years a number of county and township studies such as Merle Curti's _The Making of an American Community_ and Michael P. Conzen's _Farming in an Urban Shadow_ have suggested that by tracing a farmer's property value from one census to the next, a fairly accurate impression may be obtained of his changing economic status. To the contrary, it appears in Oregon that the differing prejudices of the several census marshals may be measured instead. Wherever possible, simple livestock and crop enumerations should be used in preference to the more subjective monetary values.

In contrast to land and equipment, livestock was the most precisely measured item of the agricultural economy. Categories were included for all the larger farm animals, which, with the exception of sizable herds, were carefully counted. Cash values were again perplexing, for while the quantities and types of animals were important considerations, so too were age, physical condition, and breed.

Livestock enumerations provide a useful example of how an objective, all-inclusive set of data such as is contained in the census can be used to check the accuracy of literary sources. In the manuscript and published literature of Oregon, swine are an almost totally ignored element of the early agricultural economy. References to them are few, and most of these are of a passing nature. Lack of substantial comment plus conflicting statements lend credence to the common belief that the hog must have occupied a minor place in the order of things. Yet, when census figures are tabulated it is discovered that swine were more common than cattle and almost eight times as numerous as the territory's famous sheep.

Because of the more abstract nature of the measurements, crop estimates were subject to greater error and should be considered only close approximations. Crops, especially the grains, proved to be useful indicators in determining the degree to which the settlement process had visibly altered the land. A herdsman with hundreds of animals might leave few lasting traces of his occupance, but the cultivator had to construct buildings and fences and break the sod.

Computerization and analysis of the census was merely the first step in reconstructing the frontier landscape of 1850. Equally important was the accumulation of cartographic materials adequate for the

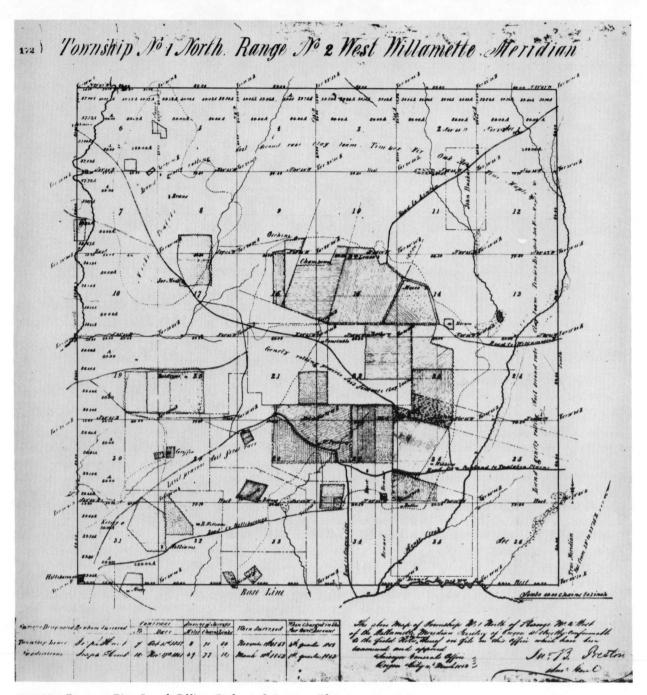

MAP 45. Oregon City Land Office Cadastral Survey Plat

production of accurate maps. No published map was of any value. All were too small or badly distorted. As a result, exclusive use was made of the archives of the United States surveyor general deposited in the Portland office of the Bureau of Land Management, the Seattle center of the National Archives and Records Service, and the Oregon State Archives.

Through custom and later through laws enacted by the provisional and federal governments, private settlers in Oregon were allowed to claim up to 640 acres of free land from the public domain prior to 1855. To regulate the donation land claims a procedure of application and certification was adopted. Among the records which resulted were three that proved especially useful. The first of these consisted of the Donation Land Certificates held by the National Archives and Records Service. The certificates include among other items the claim number, recipient's name, his birthplace by county and state, his birthdate, date and place of marriage, date arrived in Oregon, official date of claim settlement, plus witnesses' signatures. The official date of settlement was particularly important, for it determined whether or not a man enumerated in the 1850 census could be assigned to a claim by that date.[3]

The second record group used extensively for establishing the locations of rural settlement was the collection of township plats of Oregon City's federal land office. These maps indicate the boundaries of the donation land claims with their acreage and owners' names.

The third and most important source of locational data was the original cadastral surveys of the United States General Land Office. Without doubt, these contain the single most comprehensive and accurate cartographic record of the Oregon frontier. The large scale township maps were drawn from field surveys made during the 1850s; and include an astonishingly complete view of the physical and cultural landscapes. Topography, streams, and the boundaries between the prairie and forest are shown, as are the qualities of the soil and the general character of the woodlands. Roads, Indian trails, towns, ferries, mills, farmsteads (with their owners usually identified), fences, plowed fields, churches, and schools are among the cultural features indicated (map 45).

Through a combination of the information contained within the above three sources with that obtained from literary records and the census, approximately 78 percent of the frontier's rural population enumerated in 1850 was located exactly on 1:62,500 topographical maps of the United States Geological Survey. Together the locations formed a network of absolute points into which the remaining households were interpolated by dwelling number. In most areas, the density of fixed locations was such that, when combined with topographical data and other historical material, another 15 percent the rural inhabitants could be located within one and one half miles of their true position. Seven percent could not be located except within the settled districts of the proper counties.

As table 9 indicates, mapping accuracy varied a great deal from one county to the next. In general it may be noted that reliability was greatest in agricultural counties and least in those possessing highly mobile populations dominated by adult males. Hence, in Benton and Yamhill counties 98 percent of the rural people can be located exactly or within one and one half miles of their actual position, while in Clatsop and Clackamas counties the record is a more dismal 71 and 88 percent. In Clatsop County, the low reliability results from itinerant gangs of loggers. In Clackamas County, it is at least partially related to the fall influx of immigrants.

Urban population was slightly more difficult to articulate and map, for locational data were less complete. With few exceptions no special notations were included in the manuscript schedules to indicate town boundaries. Furthermore, published volumes of the census list only five of at least nine recognizable towns and compound the error by giving each a demonstrably wrong total. The best indicator of a town was the diverse occupational structure of the urban population which contrasted greatly to that of the farmer-dominated rural districts. When combined with a sudden absence of donation land claim recipients in the census schedules, the townspeople could be identified. In most cases, town populations could be estimated within 10 percent of their true figure by corroborating them with donation land claimants. Only in Clackamas County with its newly arrived immigrants and less than perfect census marshal was there any real difficulty.

TABLE 9

MAP LOCATION ACCURACY OF RURAL POPULATION

County	Total Population	Persons Located Exactly		Households Located Exactly		Persons Located Closely		Households Located Closely		Persons Located Poorly		Households Located Poorly	
		%	No.	%	No.	%	No.	%	No.	%	No.	%	No.
Benton	803	90.78	729	84.67	127	7.84	63	13.33	20	1.38	11	2.00	3
Clackamas	759	76.67	582	61.02	108	10.80	82	11.86	21	12.53	95	27.12	48
Clatsop	241	52.28	126	32.65	16	18.67	45	26.53	13	29.05	70	40.82	20
Linn	987	83.49	824	81.50	141	9.83	97	12.14	21	6.68	66	6.36	11
Marion	2,409	75.55	1,820	70.31	315	15.86	382	19.87	89	8.59	207	9.82	44
Polk	1,043	79.58	830	74.21	141	16.30	170	19.47	37	4.12	43	6.32	12
Washington	1,485	73.26	1,088	62.60	154	18.25	271	19.92	48	8.49	126	17.48	42
Yamhill	1,357	70.59	1,080	76.89	173	18.13	246	20.89	47	2.28	31	2.22	5
Oregon	9,084	77.93	7,079			14.93	1,356						

Notes

CHAPTER 2

1. Peter H. Burnett, "Recollections of the Past," Bancroft Library ms. P-A 12, p. 97.

2. Matthew P. Deady, "History and Progress of Oregon after 1845," Bancroft Library ms. P-A 24, p. 59.

3. J. H. Baxter for the Secretary of War, *Statistics, Medical and Anthropological, of the Provost-Marshall General's Bureau*, 1:389.

4. Ralph C. Geer, "The Pioneer Nurseryman in the Waldo Hills," Bancroft Library ms. P-A 35, p. 2.

5. Henry R. Schoolcraft, "A Journey Up The Illinois River In 1821" in Milo Quaife, ed., *Pictures of Illinois One Hundred Years Ago*, p. 86.

6. Peter H. Burnett, *Recollections and Opinions of an Old Pioneer*, p. 98.

7. John Ball, letter dated 29 April 1832, Lexington, Missouri, in the *Christian Advocate and Journal* (New York, 1 December 1833).

CHAPTER 3

1. T. L. Davidson, "By the Southern Route into Oregon," Bancroft Library ms. P-A 23, p. 1.

2. Solomon Zumwalt, "The Biography of Adam Zumwalt," Bancroft Library ms. P-A 337:10, p. 16.

3. Joel Palmer, "Conducting the Wagon Trains Flanking Mt. Hood and Cariboo," Bancroft Library ms. P-A 58, p. 25.

4. William Strong, "History of Oregon," Bancroft Library ms. P-A 68, p. 19.

CHAPTER 4

1. George B. Roberts, "Recollections," Bancroft Library ms. P-A 83, p. 38.

2. David Douglas, *Journal kept by David Douglas during his travels in North America, 1823–27*, p. 213.

3. Jason Lee, extracts from the journal of Rev. Jason Lee published in the *Christian Advocate and Journal* (New York, 25 August 1841).

4. Jesse A. Applegate, "Settlement of Polk County," in Joseph H. Brown, "Oregon Miscellanies," Bancroft Library ms. P-A 9, p. 14.

5. James Clyman, "Diary," 11 December 1844, in *James Clyman, American Frontiersman*, ed. Charles Camp, p. 121.

CHAPTER 5

1. Daniel Waldo, "Critiques," Bancroft Library ms. P-A 74, pp. 15–16.

2. John McLoughlin, "Private Papers: 1825–1856," Bancroft Library ms. P-A 155:2, pp. 19–20.

3. Peter H. Burnett, "Recollections of the Past," Bancroft Library ms. P-A 12, p. 167.

4. Ibid., p. 159–61.

5. Waldo, "Critiques," p. 7.

6. John M. Bacon, "Mercantile Life at Oregon City," Bancroft Library ms. P-A 4, pp. 9–10.

7. Robert Earl, "Reminiscences," Oregon Historical Society ms. 669, pp. 12–14.

8. William Shaw, "Pioneer Life," Bancroft Library ms. P-A 64, p. 15. Alvin T. Smith, "Daybook and Diary," Oregon Historical Society ms. 8, 21 March 1845.

9. Burnett, "Recollections," p. 158–59.

10. Neil M. Howison, *Report of Lieutenant Neil M. Howison*.

11. Philip L. Edwards, "A Sketch of Oregon Territory or the Emigrant's Guide," Bancroft Library ms. P-A 29, p. 27.

12. Oregon (State), *The Organic and Other General Laws of Oregon, 1845–1864*, pp. 63–64.

13. Oregon (Territorial government), *Laws of a General and Local Nature—Legislative Assemblies 1843–49*, pp. 77–78.

14. Ibid., p. 72.

15. Horace Holden, "Oregon Pioneering," Bancroft Library ms. P-A 40, p. 2.

16. *Oregon Spectator*, 30 September 1847.

CHAPTER 6

1. Peter H. Burnett, "Recollections of the Past," Bancroft Library ms. P-A 12, p. 176.

2. William Strong, "History of Oregon," Bancroft Library ms. P-A 68, p. 61.

3. Lincoln Wilkes, *By an Oregon Pioneer Fireside*, pp. 65–66.

4. Alvin T. Smith, "Daybook and Diary," Oregon Historical Society ms. 8, 1842–45.

5. *Oregon Spectator*, 4 February 1847.

6. Robert Earl, "Reminiscences," Oregon Historical Society ms. 669, p. 30.

7. Sydney Moss, "Pictures of Pioneer Times at Oregon City," Bancroft Library ms. P-A 124, p. 26.

8. Martha Minto, "Female Pioneering in Oregon," Bancroft Library ms. P-A 51, p. 25.

9. Daniel Waldo, "Critiques," Bancroft Library ms. P-A 74, p. 11.

10. Smith, "Diary," 1842–48.

CHAPTER 7

1. John McLoughlin, "Private Papers: 1825–1856," Bancroft Library ms. P-A 155:2, p. 1.

2. James Clyman, "Diary," 15 January 1845, in *James Clyman, American Frontiersman*, ed. Charles Camp, pp. 133–34.

3. Hubert H. Bancroft, *History of Oregon*, 2:448.

4. William Strong, "History of Oregon," Bancroft Library ms P-A 68, p. 17.

5. Joel Palmer, *Journal of Travels*, p. 257.

6. Joseph H. Brown, "Settlement of the Willamette Valley," Bancroft Library ms. P-A 10, p. 6.

7. Robert R. Thompson, "Statement, 1884," Bancroft Library ms. P-A 117, p. 7.

8. George B. Roberts, "Recollections," Bancroft Library ms. P-A 83, p. 45.

9. Joseph Watt, "First Things," Bancroft Library ms. P-A 75, p. 7.

10. Nathaniel Wyeth, "Memoir, Cambridge, February 4, 1839," p. 15.

11. Joel Palmer to Indian Commissioner George Manypenny, 21 March 1854, published in part in Charles H. Carey, *History of Oregon*, 1:580–81.

12. Charles Wilkes, *Narrative of the United States Exploring Expedition,* 4:355.

13. Philip L. Edwards, "A Sketch of Oregon Territory, or the Emigrant's guide," Bancroft Library ms. P-A 29, p. 27.

14. Neil M. Howison, Report of Lieutenant Neil M. Howison, p. 29.

15. Peter Crawford, "Narrative of the Overland Journey to Oregon," Bancroft Library ms. P-A 20, p. 164.

16. Peter H. Burnett, "Recollections of the Past," Bancroft Library ms. P-A 12, pp. 183–84.

17. Ralph C. Geer, "The Pioneer Nurseryman in the Waldo Hills," Bancroft Library ms. P-A 35, p. 4.

APPENDIX

1. The census was conducted under the direction of Joseph L. Meek, United States marshal of Oregon Territory. Besides Meek, who enumerated Clackamas County between September 6 and October 26, there were three assistants: Daniel O'Niell, who canvassed Linn County (September 8 to 21), Benton County (September 23 to October 7), Polk County (October 7 to October 21), Yamhill County (October 22 to November 20), and Washington County (December 4, 1850, to January 8, 1851); Samuel Culver, who counted Clatsop County (February 1, 1851, to March 9, 1851); and Willard Rees, who was responsible for Marion County (December 20, 1850, to February 6, 1851).

2. Detailed descriptions of these schedules are contained in: Carroll D. Wright, *The History and Growth of the United States Census,* pp. 44–47, 147–53.

3. Because of the voluminous size and limited availability of these records general users may wish to consult instead four volumes of certificate abstracts published by the Genealogical Forum of Portland, Oregon (see bibliography).

Bibliography

PRIMARY SOURCES

MANUSCRIPTS AND MANUSCRIPT COLLECTIONS

Abernethy, Anne P.
  "Mission Family." Portland, Oregon, 1878. Bancroft Library, University of California.
Applegate, Jesse.
  "Views of Oregon History." Yoncalla, Oregon, 1878. Bancroft Library, University of California.
Athey, James.
  "Workshops at Oregon City." Oregon City, Oregon, 1878. Bancroft Library, University of California.
Bacon, John M.
  "Mercantile Life at Oregon City." Oregon City, Oregon, 1878. Bancroft Library, University of California.
Barnes, George A.
  "Oregon and California in 1849." Olympia, Washington, 1878. Bancroft Library, University of California.
Blanchet, Francis N.
  "The Catholic Missionaries of Oregon," Portland, Oregon, 1878. Bancroft Library, University of California.
Bozarth, Christopher.
  "Dictation." Woodland, Washington. Bancroft Library, University of California.
Branson, B. B.
  "Settlement of Sheridan." Sheridan, Oregon, 1884. Bancroft Library, University of California.
Bristow, Elijah L.
  "Letters. 1857–1864." Bancroft Library, University of California.

———.
  "Rencounters with Indians, Highwaymen, and Outlaws." Salem, Oregon, 1878. Bancroft Library, University of California.
Bristow, John K.
  "Daybook and Ledger." Oregon Historical Society.
Brown, Joseph H.
  "Autobiography." Salem, Oregon, 1878. Bancroft Library, University of California.

———.
  "Oregon Miscellanies." Salem, Oregon, 1878. Bancroft Library, University of California.

———.
  "Settlement of Willamette Valley." Salem, Oregon, 1878. Bancroft Library, University of California.
Buck, William W.
  "Enterprises at Oregon City." Oregon City, Oregon, 1878. Bancroft Library, University of California.
Burnett, Peter H.
  "Recollections of the Past." San Francisco, 1878. Bancroft Library, University of California.
Bushnell, John C.
  "Narrative of John Corydon Bushnell, 1853." Bancroft Library, University of California.
Clark, Harvey L.
  Letter to B. Geiger. Willamette Falls, 16 March 1843. Oregon Historical Society.
Cox, Thomas.
  "Biography of Thomas Cox." 1879. Bancroft Library, University of California.
Crawford, Medorem.
  "The Missionaries and Their Work." Salem, Oregon, 1878. Bancroft Library, University of California.

Crawford, Peter W.

"Narrative of the Overland Journey to Oregon." Cowlitz Station, Washington, 1878. Bancroft Library, University of California.

Davidson, T. L.

"By the Southern Route into Oregon." Salem, Oregon, 1878. Bancroft Library, University of California.

Deady, Matthew P.

"History and Progress of Oregon after 1845." Portland, Oregon, 1878. Bancroft Library, University of California.

Durbin, Solomon.

"Dictation." Rockville, Oregon, 1885. Bancroft Library, University of California.

Eakin, Richard.

"Sailor and Saddle Maker." Salem, Oregon, 1878. Bancroft Library, University of California.

Earl, Robert.

"Reminiscences." Linn County, Oregon. Oregon Historical Society.

Ebbert, George W.

"A Trapper's Life in the Rocky Mountains of Oregon, from 1829 to 1839." Salem, Oregon, 1878. Bancroft Library, University of California.

Edwards, Philip L.

"Diary of Philip L. Edwards, from January 14, 1837, to September 18, 1837." Bancroft Library, University of California.

————.

"A Sketch of Oregon Territory or the Emigrants' Guide." Bancroft Library, University of California.

Emmons, George F.

"Letter to H. H. Bancroft." Princeton, New Jersey, 20 December 1879. Bancroft Library, University of California.

Ford, Ninevah.

"The Pioneer Road Makers." Salem, Oregon, 1878. Bancroft Library, University of California.

Geer, Ralph C.

"Blooded Cattle in Oregon." Salem. Oregon, 1878. Bancroft Library, University of California.

————.

"The Pioneer Nurseryman in the Waldo Hills." Salem, Oregon, 1878. Bancroft Library, University of California.

Griffin, J. S.

"Papers of Reverend J. S. Griffin." Pacific University Library, Forest Grove, Oregon.

Grim, John W.

"Emigrant Anecdotes." Salem, Oregon, 1878. Bancroft Library, University of California.

Harden, Absolom B.

"Trail Diary, 1847." Oregon Historical Society.

Holden, Horace.

"Oregon Pioneering." Salem, Oregon, 1878. Bancroft Library, University of California.

Holman, Joseph.

"The Peoria Party for Oregon in 1839." Salem, Oregon, 1878. Bancroft Library, University of California.

Howell, John E.

"Overland Journal, 1845." Oregon Historical Society.

Hulin, Lester.

"1847 Diary of Applegate Trail to Oregon." Bancroft Library, University of California.

Hutchinson, Thomas.

"Letter to John Butler." Polk County, Oregon, 7 March 1854. Bancroft Library, University of California.

Kaiser, P. C.

"How We Made the Emigrant Road." Salem, Oregon, 1878. Bancroft Library, University of California.

Minto, John.

"Early Days of Oregon." Salem, Oregon, 1878. Bancroft Library, University of California.

Minto, Martha.

"Female Pioneering in Oregon." Salem, Oregon, 1878. Bancroft Library, University of California.

Moss, Sydney W.

"Pictures of Pioneer Times at Oregon City." Oregon City, Oregon, 1878. Bancroft Library, University of California.

Nesmith James W.

"Reminiscences." Salem, Oregon, 1878. Bancroft Library, University of California.

Oregon Biographies.

1887, 38 items. Bancroft Library, University of California.

Oregon Dictations.
    1885–87, 46 items. Bancroft Library, University of California.
Palmer, Joel.
    "Conducting the Wagon Trains, Flanking Mt. Hood and Cariboo." Salem, Oregon, 1878. Bancroft Library, University of California.
———.
    "Early Intercourse." Bancroft Library, University of California.
Parker, Samuel J.
    "The North West and Pacific Coast of the United States." Ithaca, New York, 1883. Bancroft Library, University of California.
Parrish, Josiah L.
    "Anecdotes of Intercourse with the Indians." Salem, Oregon, 1878. Bancroft Library, University of California.
Pease, David.
    "Diary of a Journey to Oregon. 1849–1850." Bancroft Library, University of California.
Pettijohn, Isaac.
    "Diary. April 30, 1847–ca. July 25, 1848." Bancroft Library, University of California.
Pettygrove, Francis W.
    "Oregon in 1843." Port Townsend, Washington, 1878. Bancroft Library, University of California.
Rees, Williard H.
    "Letters to H. H. Bancroft." Butteville, Oregon, 1879. Bancroft Library, University of California.
Roberts, George B.
    "Recollections." Cathlamet, Oregon, 1878–82. Bancroft Library, University of California.
Ross, John E.
    "Narrative of an Indian Fighter," Jacksonville, Oregon, 1878. Bancroft Library, University of California.
Shaw, William.
    "Pioneer Life." Salem, Oregon, 1878. Bancroft Library, University of California.
Smith, Alvin T.
    "Diary of Alvin Thompson Smith." Tualatin, Oregon. Oregon Historical Society.
Strong, William.
    "History of Oregon." Portland, Oregon, 1878. Bancroft Library, University of California.
Tetherow, Solomon.
    "The Organizational Journal of An Emigrant Train of 1845 Captained by Solomon Thetherow." Bancroft Library, University of California.
Thompson, Robert.
    "Statement. 1884." Bancroft Library, University of California.
Thornton, Jesse Q.
    "Oregon History." Salem, Oregon, 1878. Bancroft Library, University of California.
Tolmie, William F.
    "History of Puget Sound and the Northwest Coast." Victoria, British Columbia, 1878. Bancroft Library, University of California.
Waldo, Daniel.
    "Critiques." Salem, Oregon, 1878. Bancroft Library, University of California.
Watt, Joseph.
    "First Things." Salem, Oregon, 1878. Bancroft Library, University of California.
White, Elijah.
    "Government and the Emigration to Oregon." San Francisco, 1879. Bancroft Library, University of California.
Zumwalt, Solomon.
    "The Biography of Adam Zumwalt." Bancroft Library, University of California.

GOVERNMENT DOCUMENTS AND PUBLICATIONS

Oregon

Oregon (Provisional Government).
    "Provisional and Territorial Government Census Records, 1842–1859." Oregon State Archives, Salem, Oregon.
———.
    "Provisional and Territorial Government Documents, 1837–1859." Oregon State Archives, Salem, Oregon.

————.

    "Provisional Government Land Claim Records." Oregon State Archives, Salem, Oregon.

Oregon (Territorial Government).

    Laws, General and Special, Passed by the Territorial Legislative Assemblies, 1850–59. Oregon City, Oregon, 1851; Salem, Oregon, 1852–59.

————.

    Laws of a General and Local Nature—Legislative Assemblies, 1843–49. Salem, Oregon, 1853.

————.

    Oregon Archives—Including the Journals, Governor's Messages, and Public Papers of Oregon, 1843–49. Compiled by LaFayette Grover. Salem, Oregon, 1855.

Oregon (State).

    The Organic and Other General Laws of Oregon, 1843–1872. Compiled and edited by M. P. Deady, Salem, Oregon, 1874.

United States

Baxter, J. H.

    Statistics, Medical and Anthropological, of the Provost-Marshal-General's Bureau. 2 vols. Washington, D.C., 1875.

Coolidge, Richard H.

    Statistical Report on the Sickness and Mortality in the Army of the United States. 34th Cong., 1st sess., Senate Ex. Doc. 96.

Couch, James F.

    "The Toxic Constituent of Rickweed or White Snakeroot." *Journal of Agricultural Research* 35 (1927): 547–76.

Gates, Paul.

    History of Public Land Law Development. Washington, D.C., 1968.

Howison, Neil M.

    Report of Lieutenant Neil M. Howison, United States Navy, to the commander of the Pacific Squadron; Being the result of an examination in the year 1846 of the coast, harbors, rivers, soil, productions, climate and population of the Territory of Oregon. 30th Cong., 1st sess., House of Representatives Miscellaneous Document 29.

Humphreys, Captain A. A., and Abbot, H. L.

    Report upon the Physics and Hydraulics of the Mississippi River. Washington, D.C., 1876.

Lawson, Surgeon General Thomas.

    Statistical Report on the Sickness and Mortality in the Army of the United States from January 1839 to January 1855. Washington, D.C., 1856. Also published as Senate Ex. Doc. 96, 34th Cong., 1st sess.

Slacum, William A.

    Report of Lieutenant William A. Slacum. Washington, D.C., 1837. 25th Cong., 2nd sess., Senate Ex. Doc. 24.

United States, Bureau of Indian Affairs.

    "Sketch of the Willamette Valley, showing the purchases and reservations made by the Board of Commissioners, appointed to treat with the Indians of Oregon, April and May 1851 prepared by George Gibbs and Edmund A. Starling." National Archives and Records Service, Washington, D.C.

United States, Census Office.

    Mortality Statistics of the Seventh Census of the United States, 1850. Compiled by J. D. B. De Bow. Washington, D.C., 1855.

United States, Census Office, Seventh Census (1950).

    "Population Schedule." National Archives and Records Service, Washington, D.C.

————.

    "Special Schedules." Oregon State Archives, Salem, Oregon.

United States, Census Office.

    Statistical view of the United States, embracing its territory, population—white, free colored, and slave—moral and social condition, industry, property, and revenue; the detailed statistics of cities, towns, and counties; being a compendium of the seventh census, to which are added the results of every previous census, beginning with 1790, in comparative tables, with explanatory and illustrative notes, based upon the schedules and other official sources of information. Compiled by J. D. B. De Bow, Washington, D.C., 1854.

United States, General Land Office.

    Instructions to the Surveyor General of Oregon; being a manual for field operations. Washington, D.C., 1851.

————.

    "Original Township Surveys." National Archives and Records Service, Washington, D.C.

——.

"Plats of Oregon City Office Donation Land Claims." Oregon State Archives, Salem, Oregon.

——.

"Surveyors' Notebooks." Bureau of Land Management, Portland, Oregon.
United States, Office of the Chief of Engineers.
"Fourth Section U.S. Military Road from Astoria to Salem Surveyed by Lieut. G. H. Derby, U.S. Topographical Engineers, October, 1855. From Harper's to Salem." National Archives and Records Service, Washington, D.C.
Wright, Carroll D.
The History and Growth of the United States Census. Washington, D.C., 1900. 56th Cong., 1st sess., Senate Doc. 194.
Wyeth, Nathaniel.
"Memoir, Cambridge, February 4, 1839." House of Representatives Supplemental Report, 16 February 1939. 25th Cong., 3rd sess., H. Rept. 101.

PRINTED DIARIES, REMINISCENCES, AND COLLECTIONS OF LETTERS

Applegate, Jesse.
"A Day with the Cow Column in 1843." *Quarterly of the Oregon Historical Society* 1(1900): 371–83.
Applegate, Lindsay.
"Notes and Reminiscences of Laying Out and Establishing the Old Emigrant Road into Southern Oregon in the Year 1846." *Quarterly of the Oregon Historical Society* 22(1921): 12–45.
Bagley, Clarence B.
"Crossing the Plains, 1850." *Washington Historical Quarterly* 13(1922): 163–80.
Barlow, William.
"Reminiscences of Seventy Years." *Quarterly of the Oregon Historical Society* 13(1912): 240–86.
Boardman, John.
"Journal of John Boardman. An Overland Journey from Kansas to Oregon in 1843." *Utah Historical Quarterly* 2(1929): 99–121.
Burnett, Peter H.
Recollections and Opinions of an Old Pioneer. New York: D. Appleton & Co., 1880.
Carey, Charles H., ed.
"Methodist Annual Reports Relative to the Willamette Mission (1834–1848)." *Quarterly of the Oregon Historical Society* 23(1922): 303–64.

——.

"The Mission Record Book of the Methodist Episcopal Church, Willamette Station, Oregon Territory, North America, Commenced 1834." *Quarterly of the Oregon Historical Society* 23(1922): 230–66.
Clyman, James.
James Clyman, American Frontiersman. Edited by C. L. Camp. San Francisco: California Historical Society, 1928.
Douglas, David.
Journal Kept by David Douglas during his travels in North America, 1823–27. London: W. Wesley & Son, 1914.
Henry, Alexander.
New light on the early history of the greater Northwest. The manuscript journals of Alexander Henry, fur trader of the Northwest Company, and of David Thompson, official geographer and explorer of the same company, 1799–1814; exploration and adventure among the Indians on the Red, Saskatchewan, Missouri, and Columbia Rivers. Edited by Elliott Coues. New York: F. P. Harper, 1897.
Howell, John Ewing.
"Diary of an Emigrant of 1845." *Washington Historical Quarterly* 1(1907): 138–58.
Lee, Jason.
"Journal of Reverend Jason Lee." *The Christian Advocate and Journal*, 25 August 1841.
Lockley, Fred.
"Recollections of Benjamin Franklin Bonney." *Quarterly of the Oregon Historical Society* 24(1923): 36–55.
McLoughlin, John.
The letters of John McLoughlin from Fort Vancouver to the Governor and Committee, Edited by E. E. Ritch. 3 vols. Toronto: The Champlain Society, 1941–44.
Minto, John. "Reminiscences of Experiences on the Oregon Trail in 1844." *Quarterly of the Oregon Historical Society* 2(1901): 119–67, 209–54.

Morgan, Dale L., ed.

    The West of William H. Ashley: 1822–1833. Denver: Old West Pub. Co., 1964.

Nesmith, James W.

    "Diary of the Emigration of 1843." *Quarterly of the Oregon Historical Society* 7(1906): 329–59.

Penter, Samuel.

    "Recollections of an Oregon Pioneer of 1843." *Quarterly of the Oregon Historical Society* 7(1906): 56–61.

Pipes, Nellie B., ed.

    "Journal of J. H. Frost, 1840–43." *Oregon Historical Quarterly* 35(1934): 50–73, 139–67, 235–62, 348–75.

Prosch, Thomas W., ed.

    "Diary of Dr. David S. Maynard while Crossing the Plains in 1850." *Washington Historical Quarterly* 1(1907): 50–62.

Reed, Henry E., ed.

    "Lovejoy's Pioneer Narrative, 1842–1848." *Oregon Historical Quarterly* 31(1930): 237–60.

Robertson, James R.

    "Reminiscences of Alanson Hinman." *Quarterly of the Oregon Historical Society* 2(1901): 266–86.

Rockwood, E. Ritch.

    "Diary of Rev. George Henry Atkinson, D. D., 1847–1858." *Oregon Historical Quarterly* 40(1939): 52–63, 168–87, 265–82, 245–361; 41(1940) 6–33, 212–26, 288–303, 386–404.

Schafer, Joseph, ed.

    "Documents Relative to Warre and Vavasour's Military Reconnaissance in Oregon, 1845–6." *Quarterly of the Oregon Historical Society* 10(1901): 1–99.

Winton, Harry N. M., ed.

    "William T. Newby's Diary of the Emigration of 1843," *Oregon Historical Quarterly* 40(1939): 219–42.

Wyeth, Nathaniel J.

    The Correspondence and Journals of Captain Nathaniel J. Wyeth, 1831–36; a record of two expeditions for the occupation of the Oregon country, F. G. Young, ed. Eugene: University of Oregon Press, 1899.

TRAVEL ACCOUNTS

Corney, Peter.

    Voyages in the northern Pacific. Honolulu: T. G. Thrum, 1896.

Cox, Ross.

    Adventures on the Columbia River, Including the Narrative of a Residence of Six Years on the Western Side of the Rocky Mountains, among the various tribes of Indians hitherto unknown: together with a journey across the American continent. 2 vols. London: Colburn & Bentley, 1831.

Drake, Daniel.

    A Systematic Treatise, Historical, Etiological, and Practical, on the Principal Diseases of the Interior Valley of North America, as they appear in the Caucasian, African, Indian, and Esquimaux varieties of its population. 2 vols. Cincinnati: W. B. Smith & Co., 1850.

Duflot de Mofras, Eugene.

    Exploration du territoire de l'Oregon, des Californies et de la mer Vermeille, executee pendant les annees 1840, 1841 et 1842. 2 vols. Paris: A. Bertrand, 1844.

Edwards, Philip L.

    Sketch of the Oregon Territory; or, Emigrants' Guide. Liberty, Mo.: Liberty Herald, 1842.

Farnham, Thomas J.

    Travels in the Great Western Prairies, the Anahuac and Rocky Mountains, and in Oregon Territory. Poughkeepsie: Killey & Lossing, 1841.

Flint, Timothy.

    Recollections of the last ten years, passed in occasional residences and journeyings in the valley of the Mississippi, from Pittsburg and the Missouri to the Gulf of Mexico, and from Florida to the Spanish frontier; in a series of letters to the Rev. James Flint, of Salem, Massachusetts. Boston: Cummings, Hilliard, & Co., 1826.

Gregg, Josiah.

    Commerce of the Prairies. Edited by M. L. Moorhead. Norman: University of Oklahoma Press, 1954.

Hastings, Lansford W.

    The emigrants' guide to Oregon and California. 1845. Reprint ed., New York: Da Capo, 1969.

————.

    A new history of Oregon and California. Cincinnati: G. Conclin, 1849.

Hines, Gustavus.
  Life on the Plains of the Pacific. Oregon: its History, Condition and Prospects. Buffalo: G. H. Derby, 1851.
Kane, Paul.
  The Columbia Wanderer: 1846–47. Edited by Thomas Vaughn. Portland: Oregon Historical Society, 1971.
Kelley, Hall J.
  Hall J. Kelley on Oregon; a collection of five of his published works and a number of hitherto unpublished letters. Edited by Fred W. Powell. Princeton: Princeton University Press, 1932.
Lee, Daniel, and Frost, J. H.
  Ten Years in Oregon. New York: J. Collard, 1844.
Lenox, Edward H.
  Overland to Oregon. Oakland: Dowdle Press, 1904.
Lewis, Meriwether.
  History of the expedition under the command of Lewis and Clark, to the sources of the Missouri River, thence across the Rocky Mountains and down the Columbia River to the Pacific Ocean, performed during the years 1804-5-6, by order of the government of the United States. 4 vols. Edited by Elliott Coues. New York: F. P. Harper, 1893.
Palmer, Joel.
  Journal of travels over the Rocky Mountains to the mouth of the Columbia River; made during the years 1845 and 1846. Cincinnati: J. A. & U. P. James, 1852.
Ross, Alexander.
  Adventures of the First Settlers on the Oregon or Columbia River: Being a Narrative of the Expedition Fitted Out by John Jacob Astor, to Establish the "Pacific Fur Company." London: Smith, Elder & Co., 1849.
Shively, J. M.
  Route and distances to Oregon and California, with a description of watering places, crossings, dangerous Indians . . . etc. Washington: W. Greer, 1846.
Simpson, Sir George.
  Narrative of a Journey Round the World during the Years 1841 and 1842. 2 vols. London: H. Colburn, 1847.
Warre, Captain H.
  Sketches in North America and the Oregon Territory. London: Dickinson and Co., 1848.
Welby, Adlard.
  A Visit to North America and the English Settlements in Illinois. London: J. Drury, 1821.
White, Elijah.
  A Concise view of Oregon Territory, its colonial and Indian relation, compiled from official letters and reports, together with the organic laws of the colony. Washington: T. Barnard, 1846.
Wilkes, Charles.
  Narrative of the United States Exploring Expedition During the Years 1838, 1839, 1840, 1841, 1842. 5 vols. Philadelphia: Lea & Blanchard, 1845.
Wyeth, John B.
  Oregon; or, A short history of a long journey from the Atlantic Ocean to the region of the Pacific, by land. Cambridge: n.p., 1833.

NEWSPAPERS AND MISCELLANEOUS PUBLICATIONS

The Oregon Spectator.
  Oregon City, February 1846–March 1855.
  "Puget's Sound Agricultural Company Prospectus."
  Quarterly of the Oregon Historical Society 19(1918): 345–49.

SECONDARY SOURCES

NEWSPAPERS, PERIODICALS, AND ARTICLES

Albany Democrat-Herald.
  Albany, Oregon, 25 August 1948.
Anderson, Hettie M.
  "Missouri, 1804–1828: Peopling a Frontier State." *Missouri Historical Review* 31(1936–37): 150–80.

Barry, J. N.

    "Agriculture in the Oregon Country, 1795–1844." *Oregon Historical Quarterly* 30(1929): 161–68.

—————.

    "Astorians Who Became Permanent Settlers." *Washington Historical Quarterly* 24(1933): 221–31, 282–301.

—————.

    "Site of Wallace House, 1812–1814 One Mile from Salem" *Oregon Historical Quarterly* 42(1941): 205–7.

Black, Lloyd D.

    "Middle Willamette Valley Population Growth." *Oregon Historical Quarterly* 43(1942): 40–55.

Camp, Charles L.

    "Colonel Philip Leget Edwards and His Influence upon Early Immigration to the Far West." *California Historical Society Quarterly* 3(1924): 73–83.

Cook, Sherburne F.

    "The epidemic of 1830–33 in California and Oregon." *University of California Publications in American Archaeology and Ethnology* 63(1955): 303–25.

Douglas, Jesse S.

    "Origins of the Population of Oregon in 1850." *Pacific Northwest Quarterly* 41(1950): 95–108.

Drury, C. M.

    "Protestant Missionaries in Oregon: A Bibliographical Study." *Oregon Historical Quarterly* (1949): 95–108.

Dye, Eva E.

    "Boone Family Reminiscences as Told to Mrs. Dye." *Oregon Historical Quarterly* 42(1941): 220–29.

Eaton, W. Clement.

    "Nathaniel Wyeth's Oregon Expeditions." *Pacific Historical Review* 4(1935): 101–13.

Eblen, Jack E.

    "An Analysis of Nineteenth Century Frontier Populations." *Demography* 2(1965): 339–413.

Elliott, T. C.

    "'Doctor' Robert Newell: Pioneer." *Quarterly of the Oregon Historical Society* 9(1908): 103–26.

Galbraith, John S.

    "The Early History of the Puget's Sound Agricultural Company, 1838–43." *Oregon Historical Quarterly* 55(1954): 234–59.

Gregg Kate L.

    "The History of Fort Osage." *Missouri Historical Review* 34(1940): 439–88.

Johannessen, Carl L.; Davenport, William A.; Millet, Artimus; and McWilliams, Steven.

    "The Vegetation of the Willamette Valley." *Annals of the Association of American Geographers* 61(1971): 286–302.

Jordan, Edwin C., and Harris, Norman.

    "Milksickness." *Journal of Infectious Diseases* 6(1909): 401–91.

Jordan, Philip D.

    "Milksickness in Kentucky and the Western Country." *The Filson Club Historical Quarterly* 19(1945): 29–40.

Kingston, C. S.

    "Introduction of cattle into the Pacific Northwest." *Washington Historical Quarterly* 14(1923).

Lanser, Roland.

    "The Pioneer Physician in Missouri, 1820–1850." *Missouri Historical Review* 44(1944).

Lockley, Fred.

    "The McNemees and Tetherows in the Migration of 1845." *Quarterly of the Oregon Historical Society* 25(1924): 353–77.

—————.

    "Oregon Immigrants of 1844." *Washington Historical Quarterly* 18(1927): 93–102.

McArthur, Lewis A.

    "Earliest Oregon Post offices as Recorded at Washington." *Oregon Historical Quarterly* 41(1940): 53–71.

Morris, Grace P.

    "Development of Astoria, 1811–1850." *Oregon Historical Quarterly* 38(1937): 413–24.

Oliphant, J. O.

    "Robert Moore in Oregon History." *Washington Historical Quarterly* 15(1924): 163–86.

Oregon Native Son and Historical Magazine.

    Portland, May 1899–March 1901.

Oregon Pioneer Association.

    Transactions of the Annual Re-union of the Oregon Pioneer Association. Salem and Portland, Oregon, 1875–1933.

Portland Genealogical Forum.

    "Index to Oregon Donation Land Claim Files in the National Archives." *Bulletin,* 1953–57.

Sage, Walter N., and Elliott, T. C.
  "Governor George Simpson at Astoria in 1824." *Oregon Historical Quarterly* 30(1929): 106–10.
Sprague, F. L., and Hansen, H. P.
  "Forest Succession in the McDonald Forest." *Northwest Science* 20(1946): 89–98.
Stone, Buena Cobb.
  "Southern Route into Oregon: Notes and a New Map." *Oregon Historical Quarterly* 47(1946): 135–54.
Tobie, H. E.
  "Joseph Meek a Conspicuous Personality." *Oregon Historical Quarterly* 40(1939): 123–46, 286–306, 410–24.
Wardell, M. L.
  "Oregon Immigration Prior to 1846." *Oregon Historical Quarterly* 27(1926): 41–64.
West, Oswald.
  "Oregon's First White Settlers on French Prairie." *Oregon Historical Quarterly* 43(1942): 198–209.
Winther, Oscar O.
  "The Development of Transporation in Oregon, 1943–49." *Oregon Historical Quarterly* 40(1939): 315–26.
Wood, Ellen L.
  "Samuel Green McMahan." *California Historical Society Quarterly* 23(1944): 289–300.
Wyeth, John A.
  "Nathaniel J. Wyeth, and the Struggle for Oregon." *Harper's Monthly Magazine* 85(1892): 835–47.

DICTIONARIES, MONOGRAPHS, AND GENERAL HISTORIES

Ackerknecht, Erwin H.
  Malaria in the Upper Mississippi Valley, 1760–1900. Supplement to the *Bulletin of the History of Medicine,* no. 4. Baltimore: Johns Hopkins, 1945.
Allen, A. J.
  Ten Years in Oregon. Travels and Adventures of Dr. E. White and lady west of the Rocky Mountains. Ithaca: Andrus & Co., 1848.
Ashburn, P. M.
  A History of the Medical Department of the United States Army. Boston: Houghton Mifflin Co., 1929.
Bagley, Clarence B., ed.
  Early Catholic Missions in Old Oregon. Seattle: Lowman & Hanford Co., 1932.
Bancroft, Hubert H.
  History of the Northwest Coast. 2 vols. San Francisco: The History Co., 1886.
———.
  History of Oregon. 2 vols. San Francisco: A. L. Bancroft & Co., 1886–88.
Billington, Ray A.
  Westward Expansion: A History of the American Frontier. New York: The Macmillan Co., 1949.
Carey, Charles H.
  A General History of Oregon prior to 1861. 2 vols. Portland: Metropolitan Press, 1935–36.
———.
  History of Oregon. 3 vols. Portland: Pioneer History Pub. Co., 1922.
Chambers, J. S.
  The Conquest of Cholera. New York: Macmillan Co., 1938.
Chapman Publishing Company.
  Portrait and Biographical Record of the Willamette Valley, Oregon. Chicago, 1903.
Chittenden, H. M.
  The American Fur Trade of the Far West. 3 vols. New York: F. P. Harper, 1902.
Clarke, Samuel A.
  Pioneer days of Oregon history. 2 vols. Portland: J. K. Gill, 1905.
Clawson, Marion.
  The Federal Lands: Their Use and Management. Baltimore: Johns Hopkins University Press, 1957.
Conzen, Michael P.
  Farming in an Urban Shadow. Madison: State Historical Society of Wisconsin, 1971.
Corning, Howard M.
  Dictionary of Oregon History. Portland: Binfords & Mort, 1956.
Curti, Merle.
  The Making of an American Community. Stanford: Stanford University Press, 1959.

Daughters of the American Revolution (Sarah Childress Polk Chapter Number 9).
  Polk County Pioneer Sketches. Dallas, Oregon: Polk County Observer, 1927.
Daughters of the American Revolution (Sarah Childress Polk Chapter Number 6).
  Polk County Pioneer Sketches. Dallas, Oregon: Polk County Observer, 1929.
Dobbs, Caroline C.
  Men of Champoeg. Portland: Metropolitan Press, 1932.
Fagan, David D.
  History of Benton County, Oregon. Portland: A. G. Walling, 1885.
Gaston, Joseph.
  The Centennial History of Oregon, 1811–1912. 4 vols. Chicago: S. J. Clarke Pub. Co., 1912.

  ———.

  Portland, Oregon: Its History and Builders. Chicago: S. J. Clarke Pub. Co., 1911.
Geer, Theodore T.
  Fifty years in Oregon; experiences, observations, and commentaries upon men, measures, and customs, in pioneer days and later times. New York: Neale Pub. Co., 1916.
Genealogical Forum of Portland, Oregon.
  Genealogical Material in Oregon Donation Land Claims. 4 vols. Portland, 1957–67.
Ghent, W. J.
  The Road to Oregon: A Chronicle of the Great Emigrant Trail. New York: Longmans, Green & Co., 1929.
Gray, William H.
  A History of Oregon, 1792–1849, drawn from personal observation and authentic information. Portland: American News Co., 1870.
Hawthorne, Julian.
  The story of Oregon. 2 vols. New York: American Historical Pub. Co., 1892.
Hines, H. K.
  An Illustrated History of the State of Oregon. Chicago: Lewis Pub. Co., 1893.
Hussey, John A. *Champoeg: Place of Transition.* Portland: Oregon Historical Society, 1967.
  Irving, Washington.
  Astoria, or Anecdotes of an Enterpise Beyond the Rocky Mountains. 2 vols. Philadelphia: Carey, Lea, & Blanchard, 1936.
Kelley, Hall J.
  A History of the Settlement of Oregon and the Interior of Upper California; and of persecutions and afflictions of forty years' continuance endured by the author. Springfield, Mass.: Union Printing Co., 1868.
Lane, H. O., ed.
  History of the Willamette Valley. Portland: n.p., 1885.
Lockley, Fred.
  Oregon Trail Blazers. New York: The Knickerbocker Press, 1929.
Lyman, Horace S.
  History of Oregon; the growth of an American state. 4 vols. New York: North Pacific Publishing Society, 1903.
McArthur, Harriet Nesmith.
  Recollections of the Rickreall. Portland: n.p., 1930.
McArthur, Lewis A.
  Oregon Geographic Names. Portland: Binfords & Mort, 1952.
Miller, Emma G.
  Clatsop County Oregon, A History. Portland: Binfords & Mort, 1958.
Minto, John.
  Rhymes of early life in Oregon and historical and biographical facts. Salem: Statesman Pub. Co., 1915.
Mooney, James.
  The Aboriginal Population of America North of Mexico. Smithsonian Miscellaneous Collections (Washington), 80, no. 7 (1928).
Morgan, Dale.
  Overland in 1846. 2 vols. Georgetown, Ca.: Talisman Press, 1963.
Paul, Mrs. Mercedes J., and Van Valin, Mrs. Ralph W.
  Pioneer Families of Yamhill County, Oregon. 5 vols. Newberg, Oregon: D.A.R., 1953.

  ———.

  Oregon Pioneer Register. 2 vols. Newberg, Oregon: D.A.R., 1951.
Pooley, William V.
  "The Settlement of Illinois from 1830 to 1850" PH.D. dissertation, University of Wisconsin, 1905.

Quaife, Milo M., ed.
   Pictures of Illinois One Hundred Years Ago. Chicago: R. R. Donnelley & Sons, 1918.
Rawlings, Isaac D.
   The Rise and Fall of Disease in Illinois. 2 vols. Springfield: Illinois Dept. of Public Health, 1927.
Rosenberg, Charles.
   The Cholera Years, the United States in 1832, 1849, and 1866. Chicago: University of Chicago Press, 1962.
Scott, Harvey W.
   History of the Oregon Country. 6 vols. Cambridge: The Riverside Press, 1924.
Wolf, Carl B.
   California Wild Tree Crops. Claremont, California: Rancho Santa Ana Botanical Garden, 1945.
Tobie, Harvey E.
   No man like Joe; the life and times of Joseph L. Meek. Portland: Binfords & Mort, 1949.
Wilkes, Lincoln E.
   By an Oregon Pioneer Fireside. Hillsboro: n.p., 1941.
Williams, Edgar, and Company.
   Illustrated Historical Atlas Map of Marion and Linn Counties, Oregon. San Francisco, 1878.
Winslow, Charles E.
   Conquest of Epidemic Disease. Princeton: Princeton University Press, 1943.
————.
   The History of American Epidemiology. Edited by Franklin H. Top. St. Louis: Mosby, 1952.

GENEALOGICAL FILES

Genealogical Forum of Portland, Oregon.
   Portland, Oregon.
Oregon Genealogical Society.
   Eugene, Oregon.
Oregon Historical Society.
   Portland, Oregon.
Willamette Valley Genealogical Society.
   Salem, Oregon.

Index

Abernathy, George, 68
Applegate family: witnesses prairie fire, 61–62; mentioned, 63
Armstrong, Pleasant, 80
Astoria, 7–8

Bacon, John: describes rail making, 67
Ball, John: discusses Missouri settlement, 20
Barter: role in frontier economy, 67, 76–77
Belknap settlement, 46, 53
Blanchet, Fr. Francis N.: establishes St. Paul Church, 10
Brown, J. Henry: discusses oxen, 83
Burnett, Glenn O., 80
Burnett, Peter H.: motives for migration of, 17; describes immigrants, 66; notes lack of wild game, 67; resides in church, 73; digs potatoes, 90, 92

Calapooya Valley, 46
Camas (*Camassia quamash*), 87
Campbell, Hamilton: purchases Methodist cattle, 10; mentioned, 81, 85
Catholic Church: establishes St. Paul parrish, 10–11
Cattle: role in economy of, 79–83; mentioned, 10
Censuses: territorial and provisional, 13–15; federal, 15, 97–101
Champoeg, 9, 10
Chehalem Valley, 46
Chemeketa, 10
Cities: population characteristics of, 53–58
Clark, Harvey, 77
Clatsop Plains: agriculture, 92; mentioned, 10, 82, 94
Clyman, James: describes floods, 62; describes roundups, 80
Communications: role in migration of, 22–25
Crawford, Peter, 89
Cultivation methods, 74, 88–89

Dairy cows, 82–83
Davidson, Albert, 23
Demers, Rev. Modeste, 10
Disease: prevalence in U.S. of, 18–21; in Oregon, 59, 63
Douglas, David, 60

Earl, Joseph, 67
Earl, Robert, 67, 75
Earl, William, 82
Ebbert, George, 77
Edwards, Phillip, 88
Ethnicity: effect on local settlement of, 43–51

Farnham, Thomas, 11
Fences, 67, 74–76
Floods: in Middle West, 18; on Willamette River, 62
Forest, 7, 59, 62
Fort Vancouver: established 8, 79
Foster, Phillip, 92
French Canadians: settle French Prairie, 8–9; ethnic clustering of, 43; agricultural economy of, 83, 89, 90

French Prairie, 61, 94

Gale, Joseph, 76, 85
Gardens, 74, 92–93
Gay, George, 80
Geer, Ralph: health motivates migration of, 19–20; establishes orchards, 93
Geneologies, 50–52
Gervais, Joseph, 85
Gilliam, Cornelius, 81
Gilmore, Samuel, 77, 85
Gold Rush: effects on Oregon of, 15, 89–90
Griffin, John, 77
Gristmills. *See* Mills

Hathaway, Felix, 10
Horses, 83–85
Howell, John, 63
Howison, Neil, 68, 88
Hudson's Bay Company: retirement of employees of, 8–9; relation to Puget Sound Agricultural Company of, 11; assists immigrants, 65; dominates retail trade, 68, 69
Hunting, 67, 68

Immigrants: general description of, 24, 66–67; birthplaces of, 24–26; regional origins of, 29–42; age/sex characteristics of, 53, 55–58; diet of, 68
Indian populations, 59

Judson, Luis, 85

Kaiser, Thomas, 75
King, Nathan, 62, 63
Kinship: role of, in communication, 24; as factor in rural settlement, 43, 50; and creation of ethnic neighborhoods, 52–54, 95

Labor: as medium of economic exchange, 66–67
Land; as motive for migration, 18; laws, 69–72; speculation, 71; sales, 71–72; trespassing on, 72
Lane, Governor Joseph, 14
Lee, Jason: establishes mission, 9–10; recruits immigrants, 23; describes wildfires, 60; reception of immigrants by, 65
Leese, Jacob, 85
Linn, Senator Lewis: free land proposal of, 69–70
Linn City, 15
Log cabins, 73
Lucier, Etienne, 93
Luelling, Henderson, 92, 93

McKay, Charles, 76
McLoughlin, John: agricultural concerns of, 8, 79; establishes Fort Vancouver, 8; assists immigrants, 12, 65, 69; Willamette Falls claim of, 10, 70

Map making, 101–3
Meek, Joseph, 67, 75, 100

Meek, William, 93
Merchants: role as credit lenders of, 68–69
Methodist Mission: establishment of, 9–10; relations with later immigrants of, 65; and wheat, 88
Migration: early history of, 9–15; motivation for, 17–21; effect of communication on, 22–24; origins of, 24–27; and interstate movement, 28–42
Mills, 62, 63
Milton City, 16, 58
Milwaukie, 16
Minto, Martha, 75

North West Fur Company, 7, 8

Oats, 79, 90–91
O'Neill, Daniel, 82, 101
Orchards, 93–94
Oregon City: early development of, 10, 12, 65
Oregon oak (*Quercus garryana*), 87
Organic Code: effect on land titles of, 69–70
Ownsbee, Nicholas, 81, 82, 83
Oxen, 74, 83–84

Pacific Fur Company, 7–8
Palmer, Joel: describes wagon trains, 24; discusses effect of swine on Indians, 87; mentioned, 83, 93
Panic of 1837, 18
Pattern, Matthew, 86
Peas, 90–91
Peault, Achilles, 93
Peoria Party, 11
Perkins, H. K. W., 10
Pettygrove, Francis: founds Portland, 15
Pomeroy, Walter, 80
Population: censuses, 13–15, 97–101; origin of, 24–26; demography of, 53, 55–58; location of, 61, 99, 103
Portland, 15, 55
Potatoes, 90, 92
Prairies: origin and location of, 59–61; effect of, on settlement, 62–64
Predators, 75, 76, 93, 94
Puget Sound Agricultural Company, 11, 85

Rees, Willard, 101
Richardson, Benjamin, 82
Riches, G. W., 82
Rickreall Creek, 46, 50
Riggs, Washington, 80
Roads, 16, 63
Roberts, George, 59, 85

Roberts, Jesse, 80
Rodgers, Lewis, 52–53
Ross, John E., 89

Sawmills. *See* Mills
Schoolcraft, Henry: comments of, on disease, 20
Shaw, A. C. W., 85–86
Sheep, 85–86
Shelly, Michael: and census of typical family, 28
Simpson, Sir George, 8
Skinner, Eugene, 63
Slacum, William: and importation of cattle, 79; mentioned, 83, 85, 86
Smith, Alvin T.: diary of, 67, 73–76, 87
Strong, William: characterizes immigrants, 24, 82
Swine: and attack fences, 76; role in economy of, 86–88
Switzler, John, 92

Tenant farming, 67
Thompson, Robert, 83–84
Tonquin, 7
Tualatin Plains: settlement of, 10, 12, 43, 61; roads on, 58

Vegetation: effects of fire on, 59–61; effects on settlement of, 61–62

Waldo, Daniel: comments on Jason Lee of, 65; poisons predators, 75; mentioned, 23, 63, 66, 82
Walker, Joel P., 11–12
Waller, Alvan, 10
Wascopam Mission, 10
Watt, Joseph, 85–86
Wheat: as medium of exchange, 68; role in economy of, 88–90
Whitcomb, Lot, 100
White, Elijah, 12
Whitman, Marcus: purchases Wascopam Mission, 10; effect of, on migration, 23
Wilkes, Charles: comments on wildlife of, 68
Wilkes, Lincoln: describes gardens, 74, 89; mentioned, 93
Wilkes, Payton, 77
Willamette Falls: and establishment of mills, 10
Willamette River, 1, 15
Willamette Valley: topography and climate of, 6–7, 75; agricultural districts in, 94
Women: mobility of, 26
Wyeth, Nathaniel, 9, 87

Young, Ewing: brings cattle from California, 79

Zumwalt family, 23–24